SIAN'S KITCHEN

CARIBBEAN COMFORT COOKING

SIAN'S KITCHEN

Carnival

CARIBBEAN COMFORT COOKING

Sian Anderson

INTRODUCTION

Welcome to Sian's Kitchen: Caribbean Comfort Cooking

Inside this book you'll find a love letter from me to you, sharing three of the things I hold close to my heart: cooking, culture and entertainment.

COOKING

I dedicate 60 per cent of *Sian's Kitchen* to my mum who, through food, created a fun and friendly environment for me growing up. I would watch her whizz around her kitchen, proudful with her pot, and see the nods of approval from her guests when they ate. I'd hear the 'ummms' and 'ahhhs' on the first taste of each dish and feel the energy in the room when dinner was done and it was time for drinks and dessert. It always filled me with pride, like THAT'S MY MUM. I should have known – like mother, like daughter – that I was going to end up like her: in the kitchen with my son peeling carrots and potatoes, reggae tunes blaring, leaning over a pot with the aroma of Scotch bonnet filling the room. To this day, she still has that same pull, that same magical energy, to bring people together solely through food. I subconsciously picked that up from her and eight years ago it led me on a culinary journey that unknowingly would see me publish 80 delicious recipes that are a reflection of modern-day Caribbean cooking and all that goes down in Sian's kitchen.

COMFORT

30 per cent of *Sian's Kitchen* is dedicated to my son Elijah (who is horrified he doesn't feature in this book, just FYI). If it wasn't for me having him in 2015 and being thrown into the depth of adulthood – moving out of my mum's house, setting up shop on my own and realising that baby needs food – I wouldn't have taken to the kitchen to become the chef that I am today. I tried to replicate my mum's cooking for me and Lij and failed because when I left home mum didn't give me a cooking manual. Every day I cooked dishes based on what I *thought* the ingredients must have been, and adapted them each time until I was happy with them. By 'I', I mean until 'Elijah' was happy with them; I will never forget when I baked salmon instead of grilling it and he told me it was slimy and refused to eat salmon ever again unless grandma cooked it. (Cold world.) I was pescatarian at the time, so it really limited my cooking options at home; I had to get better, quicky, cause baby's gotta eat!

Being a new mum and living in my own home was challenging, but cooking made me happy and, after spending all day apart at nursery or work, mealtime brought my family together. Whether it was cooking together or sitting on the sofa in front of the TV (we didn't have a dining table) and eating together, our comfort time was mainly accompanied by food.

CULTURE

Growing up in the UK but frequently visiting Saint Lucia was difficult for my palette. I wanted the flavours of the Caribbean but had to accept that some of my favourite items such as mangos, breadfruit and coconut were rarely in season or accessible in England. In the Caribbean community, it's frowned upon to not use fresh produce, but the reality is that tinned breadfruit and coconut milk are good substitutes for the real deal if you're seasoning your food well and relying on green seasonings to accompany them instead of powdered. As soon as I stopped beating myself up about substituting items you can't get easily here, I became a much better chef and was able to be way more experimental with my dishes. Rule breaking? Yes. But delicious dishes? Also, yes!

ENTERTAINMENT

Inside *Sian's Kitchen*, you'll find conversations with some of my peers in the entertainment industry who are big foodies like me. My experience in life – and as a broadcaster and DJ – is that food and entertainment go hand-in-hand. I've spent a lot of time in restaurants reasoning with my peers, at events munching on expensive canapés, or at home in Sian's kitchen, literally chopping it up with the pals – pals who are extraordinary, have extraordinary stories and careers, and who I feel are making positive changes in the world that need to be highlighted and celebrated. Thank you Big Narstie, Big Zuu and Julie Adenuga for everything you do for your communities. Legends.

You'll also find a playlist of tunes that I jam to when I'm cooking; they chill me out and get me in the zone when I'm prepping or getting ready to cook. Which leads me to my final word…

FINAL WORD

Cooking isn't always easy. It requires passion, patience and a willingness to succeed. I don't cook when I'm hungry because nine times out of ten the dish will come out wrong. I've learned to put time aside for cooking in the same way that I put time aside for entertainment, for the gym, for my hobbies, etc. Prep is also key; nine times out of ten your dish will come out right if you have read the recipe a few times over, lined up all your ingredients, gathered and washed all the utensils and pots required and are as ready as you can be.

The last 10 per cent of this book I dedicate to myself. Younger Sian would go absolutely crazy if she knew the 10,000 hours she put into reading day-in and day-out would eventually lead to her own book being published. She'd absolutely freak. So big up her!

Explore and enjoy *Sian's Kitchen; Caribbean Comfort Cooking* and share your stories with me @siananderson. I hope this book gives you a modern-day taste of the Caribbean and brings people together for you, just like food did for me.

Sian xx

Notes
Be cautious when handling Scotch bonnets; use gloves and avoid touching your face. Where Scotch bonnets are minced, they should almost create a paste, rather than being finely chopped. All salt is fine, table salt.

01

20 MINUTES

Corned Beef
aka Bully Beef

SERVES 4

1 tbsp vegetable oil
1 onion, diced
1 red (bell) pepper,
   deseeded and diced
1 tomato, diced
1 garlic clove, minced
¼ Scotch bonnet chilli,
   minced
½ tsp salt
½ tsp ground black pepper
½ tsp all-purpose seasoning
1 x 340g (12oz) can
   of corned beef
2 tbsp drained
   canned sweetcorn
1 tbsp tomato ketchup

TO SERVE
Fried Plantain (see page 38)
Avocado, sliced
White rice

Corned Beef is my earliest memory of food. Whether it was breakfast, lunch or dinner, you could guarantee at least once a week we were eating corned beef in my household. I wasn't mad at it, it's always been such a delicious and vibrant dish. Everyone adds their own sides to this dish but I am precious about how this goes down – plantain, avocado and white rice on the side are a must. If I'm feeling extra bouji, I'll add fried dumplings. Corned beef is also known as 'bully beef' and is recognised widely as 'slave food' for its history – being a tinned and salted meat that was easily preserved hundreds of years ago, like way before my time, and fed to slaves. Interestingly you can't buy corned beef for cheap anywhere in this day and age, but I do still make an effort to buy it, and when I had my son in 2015, I used to cook this and pop it in the blender for him, so that he could enjoy the flavours too.

Heat the oil in a large frying pan over medium heat and add your onion, (bell) pepper and tomato. Sauté for 5 minutes until softened, then add the garlic and Scotch bonnet and cook for another 1 minute.

Add the salt, black pepper, all-purpose seasoning and corned beef, breaking it up into pieces with a wooden spoon in the pan. Add the sweetcorn and ketchup and season to taste. Reduce the heat to low and allow to cook for a further 5 minutes until the beef is soft. Serve with plantain, avocado and white rice.

Curry Prawns

SERVES 4

450g (1lb) large prawns (shrimp), peeled and deveined
3 tbsp Betapac curry powder
1 tbsp all-purpose seasoning
1 tsp ground cumin
1 tsp mixed herbs
1 tsp paprika
1 tsp turmeric
3 garlic cloves, minced
2 tbsp vegetable oil
1 small onion, chopped
2 (bell) peppers, colours of your choice, deseeded and sliced
¼ Scotch bonnet chilli, minced
2 cloves
2 bay leaves
4 sprigs of fresh thyme
2 tomatoes, chopped
250ml (9fl oz/1 cup) coconut milk
1 tbsp dark brown sugar
1 tbsp ketchup
½ tsp salt
1 tsp ground black pepper
White rice or macaroni pasta, to serve

There are never enough curry prawns in the world to satisfy me – whenever I eat this, I wish I made more. Coconut milk and curry powder combined doesn't get spoken about as often as it should; smooth and aromatic, it takes the prawns to another level and compliments the texture so well. Yum yum yum.

Put the prawns in a bowl and season with 2 tablespoons of the Betapac curry powder, the all-purpose seasoning, cumin, mixed herbs, paprika, turmeric and the garlic. Cover and leave to marinate for 30 minutes.

In a pan, heat the vegetable oil with the remaining 1 tablespoon of curry powder. Cook for 20–30 seconds, then add your onion, (bell) peppers and Scotch bonnet and sauté until the onion is translucent.

Stir in your cloves, bay leaves and thyme and cook for 2–3 minutes. Add your seasoned prawns and tomatoes and cook for 3–4 minutes until your prawns turn pink. Add the coconut milk, brown sugar and ketchup and simmer on low for an additional 3 minutes until warmed through. Season with the salt and black pepper and serve with white rice or macaroni pasta.

Salmon Run Down
Fish in Coconut Sauce

SERVES 4

450g (1lb) salmon fillets
1 tsp ground
    white pepper
½ tsp salt
1 tsp ground allspice
1 tbsp vegetable oil
1 onion, chopped
2 garlic cloves, minced
2 bay leaves
2 sprigs of fresh thyme
½ Scotch bonnet chilli,
    minced
2 tomatoes, roughly chopped
½ tbsp paprika
500ml (17fl oz/2 cups)
    coconut milk
¼ handful of fresh parsley,
    roughly chopped, to garnish

DUMPLINGS (optional)
260g (9¼oz/2 cups) plain
    (all-purpose flour)
½ tsp salt

I'd never been a fan of fish in soups or stews, but I first had this when I was at a friend's house, cooked by her mum, and didn't have the heart to refuse. I braced myself for fish in stew, but then was so pleasantly surprised that it's become a quick dish in my house for everyone to love and share.

Cut the fish into cubes and pat them dry with paper towels. Season the fish with the white pepper, salt and allspice and set aside.

Heat vegetable oil in a large frying pan over medium heat and add the onion, garlic, bay leaves, thyme and Scotch bonnet and stir for about a minute. Add the tomatoes, paprika and coconut milk and bring to a boil, then let it simmer for 4–5 minutes.

To make the dumplings, combine the flour and salt in a mixing bowl, mixing until well combined. Gradually add up to 185ml (6fl oz/¾ cup) of cold water to the bowl, mixing gently until it forms a rough and slightly sticky dough. Add more water as needed until the dough comes together into a firm but not overly dry ball.

Knead the dough few minutes until it's smooth and elastic. Break off small portions of the dough and roll them between your palms to form small, round dumplings. Add them one by one to the sauce, being sure not to overcrowd the pot. Cook for 5 minutes.

Add the fish and continue cooking for about 7 minutes, or until fish is fully cooked. Add the parsley and simmer for 1–2 minutes. Remove from the heat and toss out bay leaves. Sprinkle with parsley and serve warm.

TIPS
+ Traditionally this is served with green banana or hardo bread which are a good alternative if you don't have time to make the dumplings.

Sweet + Sour Chicken

SERVES 4

125ml (4fl oz/½ cup)
    pineapple juice
60ml (2fl oz/¼ cup) soy sauce
50g (1¾oz/¼ cup) dark brown
    sugar
60ml (2fl oz/¼ cup) malt vinegar
4 tbsp tomato ketchup
2 tbsp vegetable oil
4 boneless, skinless chicken
    breasts, cut into chunks
1 onion, diced
2 garlic cloves, minced
1 tbsp grated fresh ginger
¼ Scotch bonnet chilli,
    minced
1 green (bell) pepper,
    deseeded and diced
1 red (bell) pepper, deseeded
    and diced
1 yellow (bell) pepper,
    deseeded and diced
Jasmine rice or noodles of
    your choice, to serve

I discovered this by accident while trying to make a replica of the sweet and sour chicken you get at your local takeaway. Every time I made the dish it felt like I was missing an ingredient, so I remixed it until I was satisfied and came up with my own!

In a bowl, mix together the pineapple juice, soy sauce, brown sugar, vinegar and ketchup to make the sweet and sour sauce.

Heat the vegetable oil in a large frying pan and stir-fry the chicken pieces over a medium heat for a few minutes until browned. Remove the chicken from the pan and set aside.

Add the onion, garlic, ginger, Scotch bonnet and (bell) peppers to the same pan and sauté until softened.

Return the chicken to the pan, pour in the sweet and sour sauce, and simmer for 10–15 minutes until the chicken is cooked through.

Serve the sweet and sour chicken with jasmine rice or noodles.

Stir-Fried Vegetables + Tofu

SERVES 4

2 tbsp soy sauce
1 tbsp oyster sauce
1 tbsp light brown
 or demerara sugar
1 tbsp sesame oil
3 tbsp vegetable oil
400g (14oz) extra-firm
 tofu, cubed
½ tsp salt
1 tbsp ground black pepper
½ tsp paprika
½ tsp chilli powder
2 garlic cloves, minced
450g (1lb/4 cups) chopped
 mixed vegetables, such as
 broccoli, (bell) peppers,
 mangetout (snow peas),
 carrots
¼ handful of fresh coriander,
 to garnish (optional)
Rice or noodles of your choice,
 to serve

**When I used to be vegan, tofu was my go-to meat substitute. This was the first dish I experimented with as I knew I loved a good stir fry. Even being a meat eater again, I revert back to this dish on the days I fancy a veg-heavy dish and it does the job every time.
If you're making this for a vegetarian or vegan, make sure you use a vegan oyster sauce.**

In a bowl, combine the soy sauce, oyster sauce, brown sugar and sesame oil to make the stir-fry sauce. Set aside.

In a large wok or frying pan, heat 2 tbsp of the vegetable oil over high heat. Add the tofu, season with the salt, black pepper, paprika and chilli powder, and stir-fry until it's lightly browned on all sides. Remove the tofu from the pan and set aside.

To the same pan, add the remaining oil, garlic and chopped vegetables. Stir-fry for a few minutes until the vegetables are tender but still with a little bite. Return the tofu to the pan and pour in the stir-fry sauce. Stir-fry for 2–3 minutes until everything is well heated through and sprinkle with the coriander, if using. Serve with rice or noodles.

Kippers

SERVES 2

1 tbsp vegetable oil
1 onion, sliced
1 garlic clove, minced
1 red (bell) pepper, deseeded
    and sliced
2 tomatoes, diced
2 whole kippers, flaked
½ tsp salt
½ tsp ground black pepper
½ tsp fish seasoning
¼ Scotch bonnet chilli,
    finely chopped
Soft rolls or Fried Dumplings
    (see page 34), to serve

This was a Sunday morning dish growing up, and one I initially hated because of all the small bones in the kippers. Once I got over the bone issue (they're super soft and not the choking hazard I thought they'd be), the rich flavours made this dish the wake-up call I needed on a lazy day. Coupled with dumplings, it would send me right back to sleep feeling full and satisfied.

Heat the oil in a large frying pan over medium heat and add the onion, garlic and (bell) pepper. Cook for a few minutes until soft, then add the tomatoes. Cover the pan and simmer for a couple of minutes.

Add the flaked kippers to the pan, then season with the salt, black pepper, fish seasoning and Scotch bonnet. Cook for a further 2 minutes, then serve with soft rolls or fried dumplings.

Vegetable Curry (VG)

SERVES 4

2 tbsp vegetable oil
1 onion, chopped
2 garlic cloves, minced
1 tbsp Betapac
   curry powder
½ tsp salt
½ tsp ground black pepper
½ tbsp soy sauce
2 carrots, peeled and diced
2 potatoes, diced
1 (bell) pepper, colour of your
   choice, deseeded
   and diced
2 courgettes (zucchini),
   1 sliced and 1 diced
1 x 400g (14oz) can
   of coconut milk
1 tsp dark brown sugar

TO SERVE
White rice
Mango chutney
Yoghurt

A great dish if you're feeling Ital, if you want filling without feeling too heavy and weighed down by your meal. The great thing about this dish is that you can add as many of your favourite vegetables as you like — you're not restricted to my choices!

In a large pan, heat the vegetable oil over medium–high heat. Add the onion and garlic and sauté until the onion is translucent.

Stir in the Betapac curry powder, salt, black pepper and soy sauce and cook for a few minutes.

Add the carrots, potatoes, (bell) pepper and courgette. Sauté for another few minutes.

Pour in the coconut milk and stir in the brown sugar, bring to a simmer and then cook for 5 minutes until all the vegetables are tender and the sauce has thickened.

Serve with white rice, mango chutney and yoghurt.

Ackee Fried Rice (VG)

SERVES 4

2 tbsp vegetable oil
1 onion, sliced
1 (bell) pepper, colour of your
   choice, deseeded
   and diced
½ carrot, peeled and finely
   diced
1 Scotch bonnet chilli,
   minced (or to taste)
2 garlic cloves, minced
375g (13¼oz/2 cups) day-old
   cooked white rice
1 x 540g (19oz) can of ackee,
   drained and rinsed
1 tbsp soy sauce
1 tsp all-purpose seasoning
½ tbsp chilli powder
½ tsp salt
½ tsp ground black pepper

A secret weapon dish, this is a delicious alternative to egg fried rice. The texture of the ackee is softer than scrambled egg but the flavours do not disappoint. I make this often; it's quick and easy and an impressive dish to all.

In a large frying pan, heat the vegetable oil over medium–high heat. Add the onion, (bell) pepper, carrot, Scotch bonnet and garlic and sauté until the vegetables are tender.

Stir in the cooked white rice, ackee, soy sauce, all-purpose seasoning, chilli powder, salt and black pepper. Cook for a further 3–5 minutes until everything is heated through.

Plantain + Black Bean Bowl (VG)

SERVES 2

1 tbsp vegetable oil
2 ripe plantains, sliced
185g (6½oz/1 cup)
   cooked quinoa
1 x 400g (14oz) can of black
   beans, drained and rinsed
½ red onion, diced
1 Scotch bonnet chilli,
   minced (adjust to taste)
1 avocado, sliced
½ tsp salt
½ tsp ground black pepper
Fresh coriander (cilantro)
   leaves, to garnish
Lime wedges, to serve

I discovered this when a friend of mine went vegan. I was convinced I couldn't be converted and didn't believe there was a dish that would move me enough to turn me vegan. This one did! Who knew such a simple combination of beans and plantain could have you rethinking your whole diet?

Heat the vegetable oil in a frying pan over medium–high heat. Add the plantain slices and cook, turning over halfway through, until they are golden brown and caramelized on both sides.

In a bowl, combine the cooked quinoa, black beans, red onion, Scotch bonnet and sliced avocado. Season with the salt and black pepper.

Serve the plantain over the quinoa and black bean mixture, sprinkled with fresh coriander leaves and with lime wedges for squeezing over.

Lemon + Herb Grilled Prawns

SERVES 2, AS A SIDE OR
SNACK

2 lemons, juiced and 1 tsp of
   finely grated zest
5 garlic cloves, minced
2 tbsp chopped fresh herbs,
   such as parsley,
   thyme and rosemary
2 tbsp olive oil
½ tbsp chilli powder
1 tbsp lemon pepper seasoning
½ tsp salt
1 tbsp ground black pepper
1kg (2lb 4oz) large prawns
   (shrimp), peeled and deveined

I can never get enough of prawns. I use this dish as an excuse to buy the massive juicy ones and, combined with lemon and garlic, they make this a fresh dish full of protein. Bring it out at special occasions — it always goes down well at a picnic or summer brunch.

In a bowl, combine the lemon juice and zest, garlic, fresh herbs, olive oil, chilli powder, lemon pepper seasoning salt and black pepper. Add the prawns and turn to coat, then leave them to marinate in the mixture for 30 minutes.

Preheat the grill (broiler) to medium–high. Place the prawns directly onto the rack of the grill pan and grill for 2–3 minutes on each side, or until cooked through.

Serve immediately as a side or snack.

Steak Salad

SERVES 4

400g (14oz) beef steak
1 tbsp olive oil
1 tsp English mustard
½ tbsp finely chopped fresh
   parsley
½ tbsp finely chopped fresh
   basil
½ tbsp ground black pepper
1 tbsp salt
100g (3½oz/7 tbsp) unsalted
   butter
1 iceberg lettuce
½ onion
Seeds from ½ pomegranate
½ apple, sliced
2 tsp balsamic vinegar
½ lemon, juiced

If (like me) you love a steak and you're on a diet, the steak salad is the way to go. There are so many fruits and vegetables you can add to your steak salad, so do experiment with this based on what you fancy at the time.

Take the steak out of the fridge and leave at room temperature for 30 minutes.

In a bowl, mix together your olive oil, mustard, parsley, basil, black pepper and half the salt. Massage the mixture into the steak and leave to marinate for another 20 minutes.

Heat 50g (1¾oz/3½tbsp) of butter in a frying pan on medium–high heat and, when melted, add the steak. Sear for 3 minutes on the first side. Flip the steak over with cooking tongs and place the remaining butter on top of the steak. Baste the steak with the butter and its juices until it is cooked to your preference. Remove from the pan and let the steak rest for 7 minutes. Keep the juices in the frying pan to pour over your salad later.

While the steak is resting, place your lettuce, onion, pomegranate seeds and apple in a bowl. Combine the juices from the steak, the balsamic vinegar, lemon juice and the remaining salt to make a dressing, then pour over the salad.

Slice your steak and serve with the salad.

Fried Dumplings

SERVES 4

260g (9¼oz/2 cups) self-raising
  (self-rising) flour
½ tsp salt
Vegetable oil, for frying

These are the simplest, most effective way to make a light meal more filling. Add boiled dumplings to soups and curries, or fry dumplins and accompany them with kippers, a full English breakfast or bully beef.

In a large mixing bowl, combine the flour and salt. Mix well to distribute the salt evenly throughout the flour.

Gradually add 5 tablespoons of water to the flour mixture. Start by mixing with a spoon or spatula, then use your hands to knead the dough. Add an additional tablespoon of water, a drizzle at a time, until the dough comes together into a smooth and slightly elastic ball. Be cautious not to add too much water, as you want a firm dough.

Divide the dough into 4 equal portions and shape each portion into a ball. You can now shape the dumplings in different ways according to your preference – either keep them as round balls, or roll each ball into a rope about 1cm (½in) thick, then flatten it slightly with your palm.

In a deep frying pan, heat enough vegetable oil over medium–high heat to submerge the dumplings. Carefully add the shaped dumplings to the hot oil, making sure not to overcrowd the pan – you may need to fry them in batches. Fry the dumplings for about 3–5 minutes, turning occasionally, or until they are golden brown and crispy on the outside.

Use a slotted spoon to remove the dumplings from the oil and place them on paper towels to drain any excess oil. Serve the dumplings hot.

FOR BOILED DUMPLINGS
Instead of frying your dumplings, you can boil them and add them to stews. Use plain (all-purpose) flour in the place of self-raising (self-rising) flour. Drop them into the stew when you have 5 minutes cooking time remaining, and stir after 2 minutes to ensure they do not stick to the pan.

Peppered Prawns

SERVES 4–6, AS A SIDE OR
SNACK

1kg (2lb 4oz) prawns (shrimp),
    shell on
2 tbsp lemon
    pepper seasoning
1 tbsp Cajun seasoning
½ tbsp cayenne pepper
½ tbsp chilli powder
½ tbsp ground black pepper
½ tsp salt
1 Scotch bonnet chilli, minced
3 garlic cloves, minced
125g (4½oz/½ cup)
    unsalted butter

These need a lot of prep — the whole taking-the-poo-out-the-prawns part (yucky) and, of course, the fact that they're shell-on and you cook them, then peel them makes for a mucky experience also, but the flavours! So undisputed that it's worth all the drama.

THE NIGHT BEFORE
Cut the back of your prawn from the head down to the tail. Remove the black vein then wash the prawns to remove any excess.

ON THE DAY
Put your prawns in a bowl and season with the lemon pepper seasoning and Cajun seasonings, cayenne pepper, chilli powder, black pepper, salt, Scotch bonnet and garlic. Cover and leave to marinate in the fridge overnight.

When you're ready to serve, in a pan, heat the butter over a medium heat until melted, then add your seasoned prawns. Cover with a lid, cook for 2 minutes, then turn the prawns over in the pan. Add 125ml (4fl oz/½ cup) of water, cover with a lid and cook for a further 4 minutes until the prawns are pink and cooked through.

Serve hot, as a side or snack.

Fried Plantain (VG)

SERVES 4, AS A SIDE OR SNACK

4 plantain, peeled
6 tbsp vegetable oil

Plantain is technically a fruit but it is cooked and eaten as though it is a vegetable. It can be added to so many dishes, or just served by itself as a simple side dish. Boiled in soups and curries, or fried with breakfasts, lunches or dinners, it's so versatile. The sweeter and riper the plantain the better, so I always buy my plantains when they've turned slightly black and bruised for the sweetest finish.

Slice the plantain into 1cm (½in) thick slices on the diagonal.

Heat the oil in a frying pan over a high heat. Check the oil is piping hot, then lower the heat to medium and add your sliced plantain to the pan. Cook for 2 minutes, then turn each slice over and cook for a further 2 minutes. Keep an eye on the plantain, to avoid it burning, and once golden remove the slices immediately from the frying pan and place your plantain in a bowl lined with paper towel to soak up the oil.

Serve hot.

TIP

+ Buy bruised plantain for the best experience – you want the plantain that are mostly yellow but with a little black bruising. If the whole banana is black, you've gone too ripe; if the whole banana is yellow, it's not ripe enough!

Sweet + Spicy Prawn Stir-Fry

SERVES 4

2 tbsp vegetable oil
2 garlic cloves, minced
1 small onion, sliced
1 tbsp red Thai curry paste
450g (1lb) large prawns (shrimp),
    peeled and deveined
1 green (bell) pepper, deseeded
    and sliced
1 red (bell) pepper, deseeded
    and sliced
60ml (2fl oz/¼ cup) soy sauce
2 tbsp honey
1 tsp fish sauce
1 tsp dried chilli (red pepper)
    flakes (or to taste)

I am always trying to replicate a takeaway at home and this is one I have perfected. It's the perfect weekday dish with enough crunch to satisfy you, coupled with having a really healthy hand of veg.

Heat the vegetable oil in a wok or large frying pan over high heat. Add the garlic and sliced onion and stir-fry for 1–2 minutes until fragrant.

Stir in the Thai curry paste and then simmer for 1 minute before adding the prawns and cooking for a further 2–3 minutes. Stir in the (bell) peppers, soy sauce, honey, fish sauce and dried chilli flakes. Stir-fry for another 2–3 minutes until the prawns are cooked through and the sauce thickens, then serve.

BRUNCH MENU

Ackee Fried Rice
p.27

Corned Beef
p.13

Kippers
p.23

Fried Plantain
p.38

Rum Punch
p.175

02

OMFORTS

BIG ZUU

**FAVOURITE
DISH:**
Tortellini or
Mac n Cheese
(see page 59)

Big Zuu is a British grime MC, television personality and founder of Drip Water — his own natural mineral water brand. He started his career in a rap group with his cousin AJ Tracey, performing at radio and live sets across London and cementing himself as a very very wicked MC.

My first memory of Zuu was that he wasn't your average MC. He was super bubbly and full of character — a rare mood to come across in the grime scene, which was founded against a backdrop of poverty and oppression. While other MCs would be stood around looking seemingly miserable while they waited for their turn on the mic, Zuu would literally be jumping up and down, hyping his peers, ad-libbing their bars and generally being a good sport.

It was this character and energy that set him apart from the rest and led to him being invited to appear on radio stations, such as BBC Radio 1Xtra, and on television, where he hosts his own show Big Zuu's Big Eats on UK channel Dave.

The transition from artist to TV host is not one that is unfamiliar with the general public, but from grime MC to foodie is not something I imagine anyone saw coming.

'I'm a serious chef' says Zuu. 'When I was like 16 or 17, my house was the go-to house when I was cheffin' it up. Now it's worse 'cause everyone has an expectation of what the food is supposed to be' he exclaims, 'but when I cook, I throw down; I'm a serious chef', Zuu belly laughs.

It's hard to tell if he's being sincere, given he laughs at every opportunity. 'I'm a serious chef. I make a mad macaroni cheese. I make a roux, then I add bare seasoning, paprika, hot sauce, mustard and many cheeses'. But what sets his macaroni cheese apart from the rest? 'When it comes to whipping the roux, I whip it with love' he grins. 'I make sure the pasta is very undercooked, so it bakes when it goes in the oven, but when it's cooked, I let it set for an hour… Moretime man will just sit there and wait for me to say 'aite, it's cool' – cause you can't eat my mac till an hour's passed.

Zuu is a lover of Italian food, citing it as his favourite cuisine. 'Tortellini is the first thing I learned how to cook. The one that comes in a packet, and you boil it for two minutes. I'd heat up some tomato sauce in the microwave and them blam'. He goes on to explain that this dish was actually the motivation behind him cooking. 'I gave it to my mum and she was like 'This pasta's not cooked'. My mum used to boil it for ten minutes and it would be mad soggy and butters. So 'cause I did it better than her, she'd be upset, whereas I would be very happy and that's why I'd continue to cook'.

Food was a big part of Zuu's life when he was growing up with his mum, who is from Sierra Leone. 'Okra stew and fufu defines my childhood – my mum would make that all the time' he remembers. 'And fried rice… with onions, vegetables, diced chicken breast and seasoning. I'm very African; I grew up on rice and poultry and meat and fish, so now I want to have less of that. I try to not eat steak and red meat all the time and I like eating veg more now. I ate so much meat growing up'. He confesses.

Another dish that was big in Zuu's childhood was spaghetti bolognese. 'It was my mum's attempt at making westernised food. And it was okay', he assures himself, looking at the ceiling. 'I rarely eat it as an adult though.' Delving into the other things Zuu rarely eats is interesting… 'Anything with cucumber or mushrooms in. I hate them more

'Durian looks like jackfruit but it's not! It's called 'vomit fruit' for a reason, avoid it, never eat that in your life. I tasted it in my mouth for three days.' — Big Zuu

than anything. I think they're disgusting'. Given he hosts multiple food shows, I wonder how he gets away with avoiding those while at work. 'At work I have to eat food I don't want to eat all the time. But they're not the worst things I've come across. In Singapore, I had durian fruit'. Durian fruit is a delicacy in Singapore, but is banned from transportation because of its vile smell. 'Durian looks like jackfruit but it's not! It's called 'vomit fruit' for a reason, avoid it, never eat that in your life. I tasted it in my mouth for three days.'

In 2023, I saw Zuu was in Jamaica via his Instagram stories. It looked like he was on the best food tour of the Island. 'I wanted to stay forever.' He was down at Hellshire Beach, known for its fresh fish: lobster, bream, oysters and home-made deep fried festivals. 'The food in Jamaica is so mad', he giggles. 'I've made Jamaican food – oxtail, peppered steak, curry chicken – but I'm getting better now because I went to Jamaica. It's very easy to

make a wet rub and blend up thyme, Scotch bonnet, pimento and garlic and add herbs and dry seasonings, but that's just the first step. Cooking it requires knowledge of exactly when to add the ingredients, as well.' All facts; it's all in the timing with Jamaican food. 'That's why I think peppered steak is the easiest thing to get into if you're trying to make Caribbean food. Peppered steak doesn't require many steps: braise the meat in a specific seasoning, cook all your veg down and then you've got a sauce.'

What's next for Zuu on his food journey? 'Listen, everything: I've got Drip Water out now in Morrisons stores nationwide; I've got *Big Zuu's Big Eats* on Dave; I've got *12 Dishes in 12 Hours* out on ITV, too, and hopefully more of those jobs. I got fired from Nandos when I was like 19, cause I wiped my face with tissue, which you're not meant to do. I was mad hot, I smelled of chicken, I was sweating, so I wiped my face with tissue and my manager was like "Cool, you're fired". It was the last time I was ever fired from anything though…' he muses. I'd big up that manager, personally – first for the on-point health and safety management there, and secondly, if Zuu hadn't been fired that day, he might not have gone on to win two Bafta Awards. So, everything for a reason, eh?

Jerk Steak

SERVES 4

4 beef sirloin or ribeye steaks
   (about 175–225g/6–8oz each)
2 tbsp Jerk Seasoning
   (see page 185)
½ tsp salt
½ tsp ground black pepper
Vegetable oil, for greasing
1 lime or ½ lemon, juiced

Jamaicans love to jerk-up everything and steak is no different. We should all have our fridges stocked up with a jerk seasoning to slather on our steaks. It's bursting with flavour and the juices make a wicked sauce for your meal.

Season the steaks with the jerk seasoning, salt and black pepper ensuring they are well coated. Allow them to marinate for at least 30 minutes.

Preheat a grill (broiler) or a griddle pan over medium–high heat and lightly oil the ridges. Grill the steaks for about 4–6 minutes per side for medium–rare, or adjust the cooking time to your desired doneness.

Remove the steaks from the griddle pan, drizzle with lime or lemon juice, and let them rest for a few minutes before serving.

Lamb Stew

SERVES 4

680g (1½lb) boneless
    lamb leg meat, cubed
2 tsp Jerk Seasoning
    (see page 185)
2 tbsp vegetable oil
1 onion, finely chopped
3 garlic cloves, minced
1 green (bell) pepper, deseeded
    and diced
1 red (bell) pepper, deseeded
    and diced
1 carrot, peeled and sliced
2 bay leaves
3 cloves
350g (12½oz/1 cup) tomatoes,
    diced
1 tsp dried thyme
1 tsp salt
1 tbsp ground black pepper
500ml (17fl oz/2 cups) beef
    or lamb stock
Rice or mashed potatoes,
    to serve

This is the king of comfort food. A lamb stew may take hours to achieve, but having patience and taking the time to let your stew cook down is worth it. I have good memories of settling down on the sofa with my mum to watch Stars In Their Eyes on a Saturday night with a lamb stew. I also have not so good memories of lamb stew, as this would be the dish my mum would make when I had a toothache. Soft and easy to chew, and (according to any Caribbean elder), the cloves are apparently good for numbing toothaches!

THE NIGHT BEFORE
Season the lamb with the jerk seasoning and leave to marinate in the fridge overnight.

ON THE DAY
In a large casserole dish, heat the vegetable oil over medium–high heat. Add the onion and garlic and sauté until the onion becomes translucent. Add the (bell) peppers, carrot, bay leaves and cloves. Sauté for a few minutes until the vegetables begin to soften.

Stir in the cubed lamb and sear until it's browned on all sides. Add the tomatoes, dried thyme, salt and black pepper and stir to combine. Pour in the beef or lamb stock and bring the mixture to a simmer.

Cover the pot and let it simmer for 1½–2 hours, or until the lamb is tender and the sauce has thickened.

Serve the stew hot and accompanied by rice or mashed potatoes.

Chicken Soup

SERVES 4

4 chicken thighs (approx. 480g/1lb 1oz) halved to make 8 pieces
1 tsp salt
1 tsp ground black pepper
1 tbsp chicken seasoning
2 tbsp vegetable oil
1 onion, chopped
2 garlic cloves, minced
2 litres (70fl oz/8¼ cups) chicken stock
115g (4oz/1 cup) pumpkin, peeled, deseeded and diced
1 leek, sliced
2 sprigs of fresh thyme
2 bay leaves
3 pimento seeds (allspice berries)
1 Scotch bonnet chilli, whole (optional)
2 carrots, peeled and cut into 5cm (2in) batons
2 potatoes, peeled and diced
115g (4oz/1 cup) yam, peeled and diced
1 recipe quantity of Boiled Dumplings (see page 34) or Spinners (see page 130) (optional)

This is the ultimate winter dish and my immediate go-to if I feel like I am getting poorly. Growing up, as soon as the weather turned, my mum would put a pot of chicken soup on and raise the spice levels with Scotch bonnet to flush out the cold. Chicken soup is fun – you can fill it with all sorts of your favourite fillers, but spinners a type of Jamaican dumpling, are my number one filler for it.

Season the chicken pieces with the salt, black pepper and chicken seasoning.

In a large soup pan, heat the vegetable oil over medium–high heat. Add the seasoned chicken pieces and sear them until they develop a golden-brown crust. This will add flavour to the soup.

Add the onion and garlic to the pan with the seared chicken. Sauté for 2–3 minutes until the onion becomes translucent. Add the chicken stock.

Stir in the pumpkin, leek, thyme sprigs, bay leaves, pimento and the whole Scotch bonnet (if using). Bring to the boil and cook for 20 minutes.

Add the carrots, potatoes and yam then cover the pot, lower the heat and let it simmer for 30–40 minutes, or until the chicken is cooked through and the vegetables are tender. If serving with dumplings or spinners, add them to the soup 5 minutes before the end of cooking.

Serve the soup with the dumplings.

Pumpkin Soup
(VG)

SERVES 4

2 tbsp vegetable oil
1 onion, peeled and chopped
2 garlic cloves, minced
1.5 litres (2¾pt/6½ cups)
   vegetable or chicken stock
1 small pumpkin (about
   900g/2lb), peeled,
   deseeded and diced
2 carrots, peeled and diced
2 potatoes, peeled and diced
115g (4oz/1 cup) yam, peeled
   and diced
115g (4oz/1 cup) sweet potato,
   peeled
   and diced
1 sprig of fresh thyme
2 bay leaves
1 Scotch bonnet chilli,
   whole (optional)
1 x 400g (14oz) can
   of coconut milk
1 tsp salt
1 tsp ground black pepper

Pumpkin is the best base for a good vegetable or chicken soup. Pumpkin soup doesn't have to be a starter or side dish; you can add as many vegetables as you like to make it a full meal, for example sweetcorn, yam, dasheen, green banana or plantain. Have fun experimenting with it and adding different vegetables.

In a large soup pan, heat the vegetable oil over medium–high heat. Add the onion and garlic and sauté for about 2–3 minutes until the onion becomes translucent.

Pour in the vegetable or chicken stock and bring the mixture to a boil. Very carefully stir in the pumpkin, carrots, potatoes, yam, sweet potato, thyme sprig, bay leaves and the whole Scotch bonnet (if using) and cook for 20 minutes.

Lower the heat and continue to cook over a medium–low heat for another 3–4 minutes, allowing the vegetables to absorb the flavours.

Stir in the can of coconut milk. Heat the soup until it's warmed through. Do not boil once the coconut milk is added or it may split and look grainy.

Remove the soup from heat and discard thyme sprig, bay leaves and Scotch bonnet. Serve hot, straight from the pan.

Macaroni Salad (V)

SERVES 4

200g (7oz) dried macaroni pasta
460g (1lb/2 cups) mayonnaise
120g (4¼oz/½ cup) salad cream
2 tbsp vinegar
50g (1¾oz/¼ cup) sugar
½ tbsp ground black pepper
½ tsp salt
2 carrots, peeled and grated (shredded)
1 green (bell) pepper, deseeded and diced
1 red (bell) pepper, deseeded and diced
½ x 198g (7oz) can of sweetcorn, drained
1 red onion, diced

The fresh vegetables make this dish an elite combo – biting into the crunch of the peppers, sweetcorn and onion against the cold pasta and creamy mayonnaise. It's also a good meal for children's lunchboxes as it's eaten cold but is very filling.

Cook the macaroni according to packet instructions, then drain and leave to cool.

Make the dressing by stirring together the mayonnaise, salad cream, vinegar, sugar and black pepper.

Tip the macaroni into a large bowl and stir in the dressing, along with the carrots, (bell) peppers, sweetcorn and red onion. Cover and keep in the fridge until you're ready to serve it.

Mac + Cheese
(V)

SERVES 4

300g (10½oz) dried macaroni,
   fusilli or pasta of your choice
45g (1½oz/3 tbsp) unsalted
   butter, plus extra
   for greasing
½ onion, finely diced
1 garlic clove, minced
2 tbsp plain
   (all-purpose) flour
500ml (3 cups) milk
160g (5¾oz/2 cups) Cheddar
   cheese, grated (shredded)
80g (2¾oz/1 cup) Red Leicester
   cheese, grated (shredded)
½ tsp mustard
¼ tsp cayenne pepper
¼ tsp Cajun seasoning
¼ tsp chilli powder
½ tsp salt
½ tsp ground black pepper

I would eat this every day if I could. Pasta and cheese has always been an elite combo but adding the crispy layer on top and messing with the texture a bit makes such a difference. I do feel a bit naughty when I have mac n cheese – especially as I do usually couple it with another carb, but who's watching?!

Preheat the oven to 160°C fan/180°C/350°F/Gas 4. Grease a 23 x 23cm (9 x 9in) baking dish with butter.

Cook the pasta according to packet instructions, until it's al dente. Drain and set aside.

Melt the butter in a saucepan over medium heat. Stir in the onion and garlic, then add the flour to create a roux. Cook, stirring constantly, for about 2–3 minutes until the roux becomes lightly golden in colour. Gradually whisk in the milk, ensuring there are no lumps in the mixture. Whisk until the mixture thickens – this usually takes about 5–7 minutes.

Reduce the heat to low, then add the Cheddar cheese and three-quarters of the Red Leicester cheese. Stir until the cheese has melted and the sauce is smooth. Season the cheese sauce with mustard, cayenne pepper, Cajun seasoning, chilli powder, and the salt and black pepper.

Add the cooked pasta to the cheese sauce and stir until the pasta is evenly coated with the cheese mixture. Pour the mac and cheese mixture into the greased baking dish. Sprinkle over the remaining Red Leicester cheese and bake in the preheated oven for 25–30 minutes, or until the top is golden brown and the cheese is bubbling.

Chicken Fried Rice

SERVES 4

2 tbsp vegetable oil
1 onion, diced
2 spring onions
  (scallions), sliced
1 garlic clove, minced
¼ Scotch bonnet chilli, minced
3 tbsp chopped fresh coriander
  (cilantro)
250g (9oz) chicken breast,
  diced
1 (bell) pepper, colour of your
  choice, deseeded
  and diced
1 tbsp chicken seasoning
1 tbsp ground allspice
1 tbsp ground black pepper
3 sprigs of fresh thyme
½ x 198g (7oz) can of sweetcorn,
  drained
½ x 227g (8oz) can of pineapple
  chunks, plus 2 tbsp of juice
  from the can
500g (1lb 2oz) day-old cooked
  white rice
2 tbsp soy sauce
1 tbsp sesame oil

Rice is my thing because you can have it in so many different ways and it always makes a nutritious meal! This simple combo of rice, vegetables and chicken achieves maximum satisfaction for all of the family. You can have it on its own or couple it with a side dish.

Heat the vegetable oil in a large frying pan, and add the onion, spring onions, garlic, Scotch bonnet and coriander and sauté for 1 minute. Add the diced chicken and season with the chicken seasoning, allspice, black pepper and thyme. Cook with the lid on for 10 minutes, stirring occasionally.

Add the sweetcorn, pineapple chunks and pineapple juice and cook for 2–3 minutes while stirring frequently. Add the rice and stir in well. Add the soy sauce and sesame oil and stir again. Cook for 2–3 minutes, until the rice is heated through, then serve.

Creamy Prawn Linguine

SERVES 4

450g (1lb) dried linguine pasta
2 tbsp butter
2 garlic cloves, minced
450g (1lb) large prawns (shrimp),
  peeled and deveined
250ml (9fl oz/1 cup) double
  (heavy) cream (use soya or
  oat cream as a dairy-free
  alternative)
35g (1¼oz/½ cup) Parmesan
  cheese, grated (shredded)
½ tsp dried chilli (red pepper)
  flakes
Salt and ground black pepper
Rocket, finely chopped, to
  garnish

I love saucy dishes and pasta, so this is a frequent offering in my house. I experiment with different vegetables all the time when I make this, sometimes adding aubergines or courgettes. You don't need to go too heavy on the seasonings here because it's already a heavy dish; the right amount of salt and pepper has a huge impact on the end result.

Cook the linguine according to packet instructions, then drain and set aside.

In a medium saucepan, melt the butter and sauté the garlic until fragrant. Add the prawns and cook for 2–3 minutes on each side. Pour in the cream, add the Parmesan cheese and chili flakes and season well with salt and black pepper. Simmer for 3–4 minutes until the sauce thickens.

Toss the cooked pasta in the creamy sauce then top with the finely chopped rocket and serve.

Ackee + Salt Fish

SERVES 4

450g (1lb) salted codfish
  (salt fish)
2 tbsp vegetable oil
2 onions, sliced
2 garlic cloves, minced
2 (bell) peppers, colours of your
  choice, deseeded
  and roughly diced
1 tbsp ground black pepper
½ tbsp chilli powder
½ tbsp all-purpose seasoning
¼ Scotch bonnet chilli
2 bay leaves
4 sprigs of fresh thyme
2 tomatoes, roughly chopped
1 x 540g (1lb 3oz) can of ackee,
  drained

TO SERVE
Basmati rice
Avocado, sliced

It wasn't until I was in my teens that I found out that while ackee is the national fruit of Jamaica, both ackee and saltfish were brought to the Caribbean due to the slave trade. Sugar plantation owners imported salt fish because it was affordable protein and it's been seen by some as 'poor people's food' ever since. I still have it for breakfast lunch and dinner – this is a weekly dish at my house.

THE NIGHT BEFORE
Soak the salted codfish in cold water overnight or for a minimum of 1 hour.

ON THE DAY
Boil the salted codfish in a small saucepan of fresh water for 15 minutes then drain and set aside to cool. When cool, flake the salted codfish.

In a frying pan, heat the vegetable oil over a medium–high heat and sauté the onions, garlic and (bell) peppers until softened. Season with the black pepper, chilli powder, all-purpose seasoning and Scotch bonnet then add the bay leaves and thyme.

Add the flaked codfish to the pan and cook over a low heat for 2–3 minutes. Stir in tomatoes and ackee and cook for an additional 10 minutes on a low heat until warmed through.

Serve with basmati rice and avocado.

Salt + Pepper Chicken Wings

SERVES 4

200ml (7fl oz/scant 1 cup)
   Chinese cooking wine
1 tbsp soy sauce
1½ tbsp Chinese
   five-spice powder
1 tbsp salt
1 tbsp ground black pepper
1 tsp chilli powder
1 tbsp paprika
1kg (2lb 4oz) chicken wings
1 egg, beaten
200g (7oz)
   cornflour (cornstarch)
1.5–2 litres (52–70fl oz/
   6–8 cups) vegetable oil,
   to deep fry
1 tbsp sesame oil
1 large onion, diced
2 spring onions (scallions),
   diced
1 tbsp minced fresh ginger
2 garlic cloves, minced
1 green chilli, sliced
1 yellow chilli, sliced

Who doesn't love salt and pepper wings? Crispy on the outside and soft and juicy inside, they make great party bites but are also briliant to cook on a Monday and snack on throughout the week.

In a large bowl, combine the Chinese cooking wine, soy sauce, Chinese five-spice powder, salt, black pepper, chilli powder and paprika. Add the chicken wings to the bowl and turn to coat in the marinade. Leave to marinate for at least 30 minutes.

Dip the marinated chicken wings into the beaten egg, then dip into the cornflour to coat each wing.

Pour the vegetable oil into a deep pan or fryer and heat it to make sure the oil is piping hot. Add a third of the chicken wings to the pan carefully and fry for 10 minutes, until cooked through and golden brown, reducing the heat to medium after 4 minutes, so that the wings don't burn. Remove from the pan and drain on a plate lined with paper towels to drain the excess oil. Repeat, frying in batches until all of the wings are cooked.

Heat the sesame oil in a frying pan over low heat and add the onion, spring onions, ginger, garlic and chillies and sauté for 2 minutes until soft. Toss your cooked wings in this mixture until all of your wings are covered. Season with more salt and black pepper to taste and serve.

Beef Patties

MAKES 6

FOR THE PATTY PASTRY
340g (11¾oz/2½ cups) plain
    (all-purpose) flour, plus
    extra for dusting
½ tsp salt
½ tsp ground turmeric
225g (8oz/1 cup) cold unsalted
    butter, cubed
125ml (4½fl oz/½ cup)
    ice-cold water

FOR THE BEEF FILLING
2 tbsp vegetable oil
1 onion, chopped
2 garlic cloves, minced
2 red (bell) peppers, deseeded
    and finely diced
1 spring onion (scallion),
    chopped
450g (1lb) minced (ground) beef
1 tsp Betapac curry powder
½ tsp ground turmeric
½ tbsp paprika
½ tsp cayenne pepper
¼ tbsp chilli powder
½ tsp salt
1 tbsp ground black pepper
125ml (4½fl oz/½ cup)
    beef stock
1 tsp fresh thyme leaves

There are so many variations of the patty – chicken, salt fish, vegetable, and so on – but nothing comes close to the beef patty. The juices, textures and flavours are just correct. People add cheese to their beef patties but I just think that's criminal – the beef patty in all its simpleness is excellent as it is. It is a very filling dish, so best had as a snack between mealtimes.

For the pastry, put the flour, salt, turmeric and butter in a blender. Blitz to make a dough, adding enough of the water just until your pastry combines into a ball. Knead it briefly, then cover and store in the fridge until needed. Preheat the oven to 170°C fan/190°C/375°F/Gas 5 and line a baking tray with baking parchment.

To make the filling, heat the vegetable oil in a large frying pan over a medium–high heat and sauté the onion and garlic until soft. Add the (bell) peppers, spring onion and beef mince and cook until the beef is browned. Stir in the Betapac curry powder, turmeric, paprika, cayenne pepper, chilli powder, salt, and black pepper. Pour in the beef stock, add the thyme and simmer until the mixture thickens, around 2 minutes.

Roll out pastry dough on a lightly floured surface. Use a 8cm (3in) round cutter to stamp out 6 circles and fill with the beef mixture. Fold over and seal in half moon shapes, crimping the edges with the tines of a fork to create patties.

Place the patties on the prepared tray and bake in a preheated oven for 20–25 minutes, or until golden brown.

Tuna Pasta Bake

SERVES 4

500g (1lb 2oz) dried fusilli pasta
1 leek, sliced
125ml (4fl oz/½ cup) milk
125g (4½oz) unsalted butter
200g (7oz/2¼ cups) mature
   Cheddar cheese, grated
   (shredded), plus an optional
   extra handful for the top
½ tsp salt
½ tsp ground black pepper
½ tsp all-purpose seasoning
½ tsp paprika
2 x 145g (5oz) cans of tuna in
   spring water or brine, drained
1 tbsp chopped fresh parsley

This was one of the first dishes I learned to make because it was just so delicious. This was an after-school snack for me to take up to my room and munch on while I did my homework. I'd follow it with a cup of tea and some biscuits while I watched *The Simpsons* and my evening was made!

Preheat the oven to 160°C fan/180°C/350°F/Gas 4.

Cook the pasta for 3 minutes less than instructed on the packet instructions, adding the leek to the pan for the final 3 minutes of cooking. Drain the pasta and leek and return them to the pan.

Stir in the milk, butter, cheese, salt, black pepper, all-purpose seasoning and paprika and mix well. Add your tuna and your parsley and mix again.

Tip this mixture into a baking dish and place in the preheated oven. Bake for 15–20 minutes, until everything is heated through. If you like your pasta bake to have a golden top, sprinkle a handful more cheese over the top of the dish before you bake it.

Pepper Steak

SERVES 4

2 tbsp soy sauce
1 onion, sliced
2 garlic cloves, minced
1 tbsp grated fresh ginger
½ tsp salt
1 tsp ground black pepper
4 sprigs of fresh thyme
450g (1lb) beef steak,
    finely sliced
2 tbsp vegetable oil
1 (bell) pepper, colour of your
    choice, deseeded
    and sliced
2 tbsp browning sauce
2 tbsp ketchup
60ml (2fl oz/¼ cup) beef stock
1 tsp dark brown sugar
1 tbsp cornflour (cornstarch)
Macaroni pasta, to serve

I wasn't always a fan of pepper steak; when I was younger, I thought it looked scary so I avoided it. When I eventually got into it and realised what I was missing, I had every variation of it possible. I landed on pasta salad as my favourite combination – fusilli pasta, salad cream, mayonnaise and sweetcorn, coupled with the spice and texture of the steak just made sense!

Combine the soy sauce, onion, garlic, ginger, salt, black pepper and thyme in a dish. Add the beef and leave to marinate for 15–20 minutes.

Heat the vegetable oil in a pan over high heat. Add the beef to the pan, leaving the marinade in the bowl, and stir fry for 3–4 minutes until browned. Remove from the pan and set aside. Add the marinade sauce to the same pan and cook for a minute before adding the sliced (bell) pepper, browning sauce, ketchup, beef stock, brown sugar and cornflour and stir.

Add the beef back to the pan and cook for another 5–7 minutes, until the beef is cooked to your liking.

Serve the steak with macaroni pasta.

Fried Chicken

SERVES 4–6

6 chicken legs or thighs
Vegetable oil, for frying
Fries, to serve

FOR THE MARINADE
2 garlic cloves, minced
1 tsp minced fresh ginger
1 Scotch bonnet chilli,
    minced (or to taste)
2 tbsp soy sauce
2 tbsp
    Worcestershire sauce
1 lime or ½ lemon, juiced
½ tsp salt
1 tbsp ground black pepper
1 tbsp paprika
1 tbsp chilli powder
½ tbsp dried oregano

FOR THE COATING
130g (4½oz/1 cup) plain
    (all-purpose) flour
1 tsp Betapac
    curry powder
1 tsp paprika
½ tsp dried thyme
½ tsp garlic powder
½ tsp onion powder
½ tsp salt
1 tbsp ground black pepper

Everyone has a fried chicken recipe but I like to keep mine simple – and as flavoursome and crunchy as possible. I make this in big batches as it requires a lot of oil, but there's no such thing as too much fried chicken. Just refrigerate or freeze it until you're ready to go again, or peel the cooked chicken off the bone and make a chicken burger or fried chicken salad to snack on the next day.

THE NIGHT BEFORE
In a bowl, combine all the ingredients for the marinade. Place the chicken legs or thighs in a large, resealable plastic bag or a shallow dish. Pour the marinade over the chicken and ensure it's well coated. Seal the bag (or cover the dish) and leave to marinate in the fridge overnight.

ON THE DAY
Remove the chicken from the fridge and let it sit at room temperature for a maximum of 30 minutes before frying.

In a shallow bowl or on a plate, combine the flour, Betapac curry powder, paprika, thyme, garlic powder, onion powder, salt, and black pepper to create the coating mixture.

Heat the vegetable oil in a deep frying pan over medium-high heat. You'll need enough oil to submerge the chicken partially.

Dredge each chicken leg in the coating mixture, ensuring it's evenly covered. Shake off any excess coating.

Use a slotted spoon or tongs to remove the fried chicken from the hot oil and place it on a plate lined with paper towels to drain any excess oil.

Carefully place three of the coated chicken legs or thighs in the hot oil, skin side down. Fry for about 12–15 minutes, turning occasionally, until the chicken is golden brown and cooked through. The internal temperature should reach 74°C (165°F). Repeat with the remaining legs/thighs.

Serve the chicken with fries.

Curried Jackfruit (VG)

SERVES 4

2 tbsp vegetable oil
1 onion, diced
4 garlic cloves, minced
1 tbsp ground ginger
2 tbsp Betapac
    curry powder
½ tbsp ground cumin
½ tbsp ground turmeric
1 tbsp ground allspice
½ tbsp salt
½ tbsp ground black pepper
1 x 400g (14oz) can of
    chopped tomatoes
500ml (17fl oz/2 cups)
    vegetable stock
3 sprigs of fresh thyme
2 bay leaves
2 cloves
1 Scotch bonnet chilli
1 x 560g (10oz) can of jackfruit,
    drained and rinsed
2 potatoes, roughly diced
2 carrots, peeled and roughly
    diced
½ x 400g (14oz) can of coconut
    milk
1 red (bell) pepper, deseeded
    and diced
White rice, to serve

This is a great vegetarian and vegan alternative to curry goat or curry chicken. You get the same great flavours and the heartiness of those dishes but without the meat. Jackfruit has a brilliant texture as well, and can fill you up nicely.

Heat the oil in a large deep frying pan over a medium–high heat, add the onion, garlic and ginger and sauté for a few minutes until the onion has softened. Add the Betapac curry powder, cumin, turmeric, allspice, salt and black pepper and cook for a further 1–2 minutes.

Add the canned tomatoes, vegetable stock, thyme, bay leaves, cloves and Scotch bonnet. Simmer for 1–2 minutes, then add your jackfruit, potatoes and carrots. Cook for 20 minutes, until the vegetables are tender, then add your coconut milk and (bell) pepper. Cook on low for another 5 minutes, then serve with rice.

BBQ Ribs

SERVES 4

1 tbsp dried oregano
1 tbsp ground
    white pepper
1 tbsp garlic powder
½ tbsp paprika
1 tbsp onion powder
½ tbsp salt
60ml (2fl oz/¼ cup) olive oil
1 rack of lamb ribs
250ml (9fl oz/1 cup)
    barbecue sauce

FOR THE BARBECUE SAUCE
2 tbsp tomato ketchup
2 tbsp dark brown sugar
1 tbsp malt vinegar
1 tbsp Worcestershire sauce
1 tbsp honey

Sweet, sticky and saucy, if you cook these right, they'll melt in your mouth. You want them to be falling apart in your hands, and with a good amount of barbecue sauce to dip the meat into. Make these on a barbecue, if you can, for that smoky flavour and they are definitely one for a summer feast.

THE NIGHT BEFORE
In a bowl, combine the oregano, white pepper, garlic powder, paprika, onion powder and salt. Rub the olive oil all over the ribs, followed by your dried seasoning. Leave to marinate in the fridge overnight.

ON THE DAY
Preheat the oven to 200°C fan/220°C/425°F/Gas 7. Place the seasoned ribs on a non-stick baking tray and cover with foil. Bake for 35 minutes, then remove the foil and bake for another 1 hour until the ribs look charred.

While the ribs are cooking, stir together the barbecue sauce ingredients in a smaller saucepan. Simmer over a medium heat for 2–3 minutes until the sauce has thickened.

Brush the ribs with a healthy helping of barbecue sauce and cook again for a further 30 minutes, until sticky and tender. Slice between the ribs to serve.

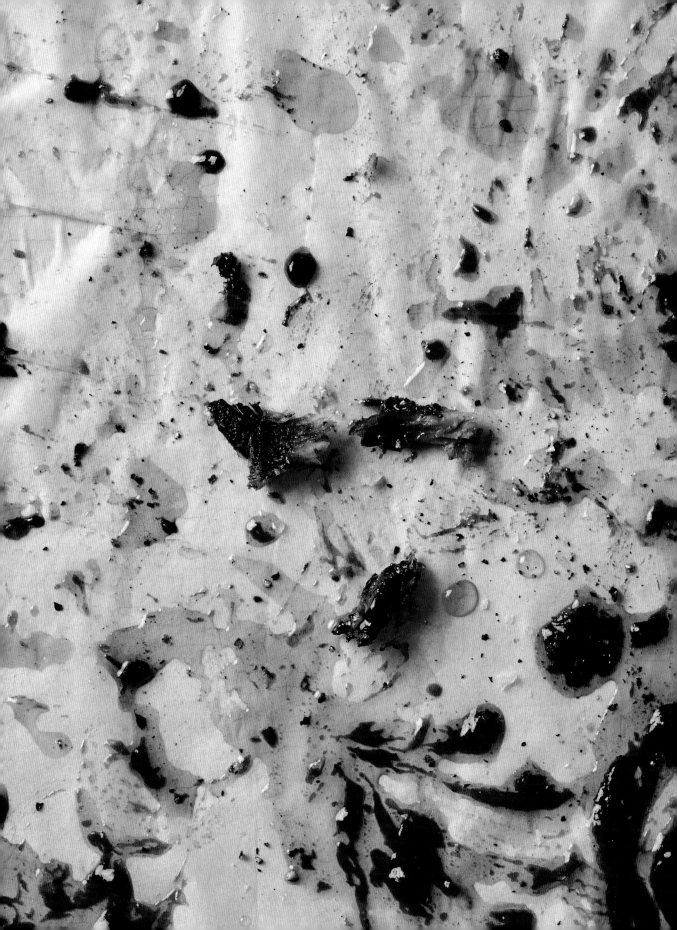

03

FROM THE ISLANDS

BIG NARSTIE

Big Narstie is an actor, comedian, TV presenter and restaurant owner, but was first known to me as an MC, specifically a grime artist. I have early memories of me in my teens discovering Narstie through his music videos on Channel U and thinking he had so much character and was seemingly such a happy fella! (Both turned out to be true.) When I began my career as a journalist at *Live Magazine*, I was in working daily in Big Narstie's ends — Brixton, London. His local butcher and fishmonger became my locals too. Even 16 years ago, being around SW9 in 2008, it was clear Narstie was a very respected member of his community, spoken about and supported locally.

FAVOURITE DISH:
Corned Beef and Rice
(see page 13)

In 2022, having been critically acclaimed at everything Big Nastie had already tried his hand at, he launched the first Jamaican restaurant in Tenerife – 'cause just like me, he is a big big foodie. When Narstie speaks to me about his early experiences of food, his story is the same as mine: waking up to the aroma of oxtail or curry goat filling the house; the familiar thump of bass lightly shaking the room, from the reggae music blasting off in the kitchen; platters of food on the dining table – a Sunday service…

'My love for food came before my love for entertaining; my belly has always been a priority and I've always grown up with good food, it's a thing I took for granted. It's only when I started to go out more I understood there's levels to what my mum and my aunty regularly cook up, it's not in everyone's household', Narstie proudly boasts.

He reminisces about meals he doesn't like: cow foot and mannish water – all delicious dishes we ate without complaining when we were younger, then grew up to find we we're literally eating the foot of a cow, the belly of goat, the tail of an ox and decided we didn't like anymore… 'I used to try and run away from the chicken foot and the tripe, and say 'Mum, you need to move forward from domestic times, Windrush is over!' We've got to run away from the trotters, pig's feet and tripe – that's hardback stuff I don't want none of that.'

So what did Narstie want? 'My favourite was corned beef and rice, sweetcorn, onions, ketchup. Put that in the ozone layer; bully beef, I'll smash that.' Bully beef (or tinned salted beef) was a food historically consumed by impoverished White people and Black slaves pre-20th century. It's not a surprise to hear Narstie cite this as a fave. It used to cost under a quid for a 340g (12oz) tin, and was a cheap, quick-to-prepare and full-of-flavour dish that would work for breakfast, lunch or dinner – a reoccurring comfort meal that would feed the whole family. In recent years the price has risen to nearly £4 a tin in the UK, so funnily enough, would be considered by some to be a luxury item in the current climate.

'The hard thing about being the Caribbean kid from Brixton who was now mingling in other parts of London, is that every shop I grew up in Brixton was Black-owned and sold coco bread and fried dumpling. When I started to go to other sweet shops and they'd have Golden Wonder cheese and onion crisps in there, it was mad to me. Where's the fried dumplings? Where's the cheesy beef patties? The experience for me feels different.'

Narstie comes from a traditional Jamaican family and is one of two boys, something he believes shaped him for the better. 'My mum ain't got no daughters and she always said, 'I'm not going to have no son depending on girls to live', so yeah, I know how to cook!' he laughs. 'I will never have to be with a woman because she cooks – I do the cooking. I ran my restaurant in Tenerife myself for the first 6 months and I did all the cooking, all the prep, the whole shebang.

I used to be a very naughty kid, so five days out the week I'd get my arse buss, then one day my mum decided to make me clean meat and fish as punishment instead, cause she knew I was scared of fish. She got 50kg of fish and made me gut and scale them. I remember that day I begged her to just beat me instead, I'd rather take the licks!' he reminisces with belly laughter, taken back to the old times. 'Now, 38 years later, I make money from the things that I thought were punishments. The life skills she gave me have allowed me to make money and be independent.'

'My love for food came before my love for entertaining; my belly has always been a priority.'
— Big Narstie

Mums, aunties and grandmas are always key figures and influences when it comes to Caribbean cooking, and Narstie's story is no different. 'My restaurant is all based off my mum's recipes, so 'mummy's special' could be her version of minted lamb, curry goat, fried fish or jerk chicken. The thing I love so much about the restaurant is bringing our culture to people who have never tried it. I had people from Moldova come over and they'd never had Jamaican food before. They hit the Jerk chicken and they knew it was mad – so much flavour. It's been a great way and place to introduce people to Caribbean foods… pimento seeds, Scotch bonnet, the sweetness of Jamaica and the special dishes my mum taught me.'

In terms of the future of food for Big Narstie? 'I have another venture called 'Jerk and Jollof', mixing Jamaican food and Nigerian food. I only just got into jollof – I was never really a fan, but my friend told me to taste it complemented with Nigerian stew and I said 'wow'. I knew then that I had to get out of having grown up in a certain way and just being used to what I am used to food-wise. You're only going to learn about something if you try it. That's what I advise everyone to do with Caribbean food – just try it.'

Vegan Trinidadian Pelau (VG)

SERVES 4

350g (12oz/2 cups) brown rice
2 tbsp vegetable oil
1 onion, chopped
2 garlic cloves, minced
1 x 400g (14oz) can of gungo peas (pigeon peas), drained and rinsed
1 (bell) pepper, colour of your choice, deseeded and diced
2 carrots, peeled and diced
2 sprigs of fresh thyme
2 tbsp soy sauce
Salt and ground black pepper

This is a dish that was first made for me by a chef from Trinidad and Tobago. It's a one-pot dish, so it's much less stress than other rice dishes and it's your chance to incorporate gungo peas, which I personally don't get to use enough. I like my pelau slightly wet, so I use more water, but if you like it dry use less water and when you turn off the heat, let the rice steam for a further 10 minutes before you take your lid off.

Rinse the brown rice under the tap until the water runs clear, then drain.

In a large pan, heat the vegetable oil over medium–high heat. Add the onion and garlic and sauté for a few minutes until the onion is translucent.

Stir in the brown rice, gungo peas, (bell) pepper, carrots, thyme sprigs and soy sauce, and season well with salt and black pepper. Add enough water to cover, then cover the pan with a lid and simmer for 30–35 minutes, or until the rice is cooked and the liquid is absorbed.

Fluff with a fork before serving.

Chickpea Curry and Roti (VG)

SERVES 4

FOR THE CHICKPEA CURRY
2 tbsp vegetable oil
1 onion, chopped
2 garlic cloves, minced
1 tbsp Betapac
  curry powder
1 tsp ground cumin
1 tsp garam masala
1 tsp turmeric
1 tbsp paprika
1 tbsp chilli powder
1 tbsp plain (all-purpose) flour
2 x 400g (14oz) cans of
  tomatoes
2 x 400g (14oz) cans of
  chickpeas (garbanzo beans),
  drained and rinsed
1 x 400g (14oz) can
  of coconut milk
½ tsp salt
1 tbsp ground black pepper

FOR THE ROTI
260g (9¼oz/2 cups) plain
  (all-purpose) flour
½ tsp baking powder
½ tsp salt
2 tbsp vegetable oil

Make sure you've got a good sauce-to-roti ratio with this – the idea is that the curry is succulent and juicy against the dryness of the bread. Rotis are a great way to mix up your curry dishes if you're used to having them with rice or potatoes.

To make the curry, in a large pan, heat the vegetable oil over a medium–high heat. Add the onion and garlic and sauté for a few minutes until the onion is translucent. Stir in the Betapac curry powder, cumin, garam masala, turmeric, paprika and chilli powder and cook for a further few minutes. Add the flour and stir until the mixture has thickened and then add 150ml (5¼fl oz/¾ cup) water and mix well. Stir in the tomatoes, chickpeas and coconut milk. Simmer for 10–15 minutes until the curry thickens, then season with the salt and black pepper.

While the curry is cooking, make the roti. In a mixing bowl, combine all-purpose flour, baking powder, salt, and vegetable oil.

Gradually add water and knead until a soft dough forms. Divide into 4 equal portions.

Roll each portion into a thin round roti. Heat vegetable oil in a pan over medium heat and cook the roti until puffed and golden brown on both sides.

Spoon the curry into freshly cooked roti breads, folding in the edges to encase the curry, then enjoy immediately.

Cornmeal Porridge (V)

SERVES 4

500ml (17fl oz/2 cups)
   coconut milk
½ cinnamon stick, finely grated
½ tsp ground nutmeg, plus a
   sprinkling to serve
2 bay leaves
150g (5½oz/1 cup)
   yellow cornmeal
½ tsp salt
1 tsp vanilla extract
4 tsp condensed milk
100g (3½oz/½ cup) light
   brown sugar

This has been passed down from grandmas all around the Caribbean and is a favourite breakfast meal, particularly in Jamaica. It's real creamy, hearty and warming. Super high in fibre, it's oozing with cinnamon and nutmeg which get your senses going in the morning.

Put 500ml (17fl oz/2 cups) water and the coconut milk in a saucepan and add the cinnamon, nutmeg and bay leaves over a medium heat. Bring to boil, then slowly whisk in the cornmeal. Allow to cook for 15 minutes while stirring to avoid lumps.

Add the vanilla extract, condensed milk and brown sugar and cook for another 5 minutes until thickened. Discard the bay leaves and serve with a final sprinkling of nutmeg.

St. Lucian Salt Fish Fritters

SERVES 4, AS A SIDE OR SNACK

450g (1lb) salted codfish
(salt fish)
260g (9¼oz/2 cups) self-raising
(self-rising) flour
2 tsp baking powder
1 onion, finely chopped
2 garlic cloves, minced
2–3 spring onions (scallions),
finely sliced
1 Scotch bonnet chilli, minced
1 tsp mixed herbs
1 tsp paprika
½ tsp ground black pepper
½ tsp chilli powder
1 tbsp all-purpose seasoning
Vegetable oil, for frying

This is a recipe I pinched from my mum and I followed it, step by step, until I had it as on point as hers. They've got to be fluffy, light, bursting with pepper and not too oily. Once you perfect these, you'll be the designated chef of your friendship group. It's the dish to bring to a party or group dinner.

THE NIGHT BEFORE
Soak the salted codfish in cold water overnight or for a minimum of 5 hours.

ON THE DAY
Boil the salted codfish in a small saucepan of fresh water for 15 minutes then drain and set aside to cool. When cool, flake the salted codfish.

In a large mixing bowl, combine the flaked salted codfish, flour, baking powder, onion, garlic, spring onions, Scotch bonnet, mixed herbs, paprika, black pepper, chilli powder and all-purpose seasoning.

Gradually add 125ml (4fl oz/½ cup) water to the mixture, 50ml (1¾fl oz) at a time, stirring continuously, until you have a thick batter.

Cover with cling film (plastic wrap) and leave to rest at room temperature for 30 minutes.

Pour vegetable oil into a deep skillet or frying pan, so that it comes 5–7.5cm (2–3in) up the sides, and heat over medium–high heat until it reaches around 180°C/350°F. Using a tablespoon or an ice cream scoop, carefully drop portions of the salted codfish batter into the hot oil. Be careful not to overcrowd the pan – you will need to cook them in batches.

Fry the fritters for about 3–4 minutes on each side, or until they are golden brown and crispy. Use a slotted spoon to remove the fritters from the hot oil and place them on a plate lined with paper towels to drain any excess oil.

Repeat the frying process until all the batter is used, making sure the oil returns to the right temperature between each batch.

Serve the fritters hot from the pan.

St. Lucian Vegan Fritters (VG)

SERVES 4, AS A SIDE OR SNACK

260g (9¼oz/2 cups) plain (all-purpose) flour
2 tsp baking powder
½ tsp salt
½ tsp ground black pepper
½ tsp paprika
½ tsp chilli powder (or to taste)
1 onion, finely chopped
2 garlic cloves, minced
1 (bell) pepper, colour of your choice, deseeded and finely diced
2–3 spring onions (scallions), finely sliced
1 Scotch bonnet chilli, minced (or to taste)
70g (2½oz/½ cup) drained canned sweetcorn
70g (2½oz/½ cup) grated (shredded) carrot
Vegetable oil, for frying
Mango chutney, to serve (optional)

Fritters are just as fun with vegetables, which make them even more crunchy and bursting with natural flavours. These are little pockets of joy that'll keep you running to the kitchen to top up your plate. Experiment to make your own version, dicing your favourite vegetables and adding to your fritter mix!

In a large mixing bowl, combine the flour, baking powder, salt, black pepper, paprika and chilli powder. Add the onion, garlic, (bell) pepper, spring onions and Scotch bonnet to the dry ingredients. Mix well to combine.

Fold in the corn kernels and grated carrots into the mixture.

Gradually add 125ml (4fl oz/½ cup) water to the mixture, 50ml (1¾fl oz) at a time, stirring continuously, until you have a thick batter.

Pour vegetable oil into a deep skillet or frying pan, so that it comes 5–7.5cm (2–3in) up the sides, and heat over medium-high heat until it reaches around 180°C/350°F. Using a tablespoon or an ice cream scoop, carefully drop portions of the fritter batter into the hot oil. Be careful not to overcrowd the pan – you will need to cook them in batches.

Fry the fritters for about 3–4 minutes on each side, or until they are golden brown and crispy. Use a slotted spoon to remove the fritters from the hot oil and place them on a plate lined with paper towels to drain any excess oil.

Repeat the frying process until all the batter is used, making sure the oil returns to the right temperature between each batch.

Serve the fritters hot from the pan, with mango chutney, if you like.

Dhal Puri (VG)

SERVES 4

FOR THE DHAL FILLING
180g (6¼oz/1 cup) split yellow
   peas (chana dal), washed
   and soaked for 2 hours
2 tbsp vegetable oil
1 onion, chopped
2 garlic cloves, minced
1 Scotch bonnet chilli, minced
   (or to taste)
1 tbsp Betapac
   curry powder
½ tsp ground turmeric
½ tsp ground cumin
½ tsp ground coriander
½ tsp ground
   garam masala
½ tsp salt

FOR THE PURI
480g (1lb 1oz/3⅔ cups)
   plain (all-purpose) flour, plus
   extra for dusting
1 tsp baking powder
½ tsp salt
2 tbsp vegetable oil, plus extra
   for greasing

This is a rare dish in Sian's Kitchen as there's a science to making it and getting it right. But if you really take care with this dish, have patience, prep it and time it properly, you'll be in food heaven. I wrap every curry in puri, from curry goat to curry chicken to chickpea curry – it all works.

To make the dhal filling, drain the soaked split yellow peas and rinse them again. Put the split peas in a large pan along with enough water to cover them. Bring to a boil, over a medium–high heat, then simmer for about 20–25 minutes, or until the peas are soft but not mushy. Drain and set aside.

In a separate frying pan, heat the vegetable oil over medium heat. Add the onion and sauté until it becomes translucent. Add the garlic and Scotch bonnet and sauté for another minute until fragrant. Stir in the Betapac curry powder, turmeric, cumin, coriander and garam masala. Cook for a few minutes to toast the spices.

Add the cooked split yellow peas to the spice mixture and stir to combine. Cook for an additional 5–7 minutes, allowing the flavours to meld together. Season with the salt, then remove from heat and let it cool. Once cool, use a fork to mash into a crumbly texture.

To make the dough, combine the flour, baking powder and salt in a large mixing bowl. Add the vegetable oil to the dry ingredients and mix until the mixture becomes crumbly.

Gradually add 236ml (8fl oz/1 cup) water to the mixture, then knead the dough until it's smooth and elastic. You may need to adjust the water to achieve the right consistency. Cover the dough with a clean cloth and let it rest for 30 minutes at room temperature.

Divide the dough into 12 equal portions and roll them into balls. On a floured surface, roll out each ball to a thin, round disc measuring about 15–20cm (6–8 in) in diameter.

Place a spoonful of the cooled dhal filling in the centre of each dough disc. Fold the edges of the dough over the filling, sealing it completely. Flatten the filled dough slightly with your hand.

Heat a griddle or large frying pan over medium–high heat and lightly grease it with vegetable oil. Place the puris on the hot griddle and cook for about 2–3 minutes on each side, or until they are golden brown and crispy. You may have to cook them in batches. Enjoy fresh from the pan.

Jamaican Curry Snapper Fish

SERVES 4

2 tbsp Betapac
   curry powder
2 tbsp vegetable oil
1 onion, chopped
2 garlic cloves, minced
1 Scotch bonnet chilli,
   minced (or to taste)
4 sprigs of fresh thyme
3 pimento seeds (allspice
   berries)
2 bay leaves
2 cloves
1 x 400g (14oz) can
   of coconut milk
500ml (17fl oz/2 cups) fish stock
½ tsp salt
½ tsp ground black pepper
2 potatoes, peeled and diced
100g (3½oz) yam, peeled and
   roughly chopped
100g (3½oz) dasheen, peeled
   and roughly chopped
1 large carrot, peeled and sliced
4 snapper fillets (about
   175–225g/6–8oz each),
   scaled and cleaned
White rice or pasta of your
   choice, to serve

Having spent a lot of my life as a pescatarian, I have always looked for new ways to season fish. Since I love curry chicken so much, one day I applied a similar method to the snapper and – voila! – it worked really well.

In a small bowl, combine the Betapac curry powder with a little water to create a paste. Set aside.

Heat the vegetable oil in a large, deep frying pan over medium–high heat. Add the onion and garlic to the hot oil and sauté until the onion becomes translucent.

Stir in the curry paste, Scotch bonnet, thyme, pimento seeds, bay leaves and cloves. Cook for a few minutes to release the flavours of the spices.

Pour in the coconut milk, fish stock, salt and black pepper and bring the mixture to a gentle simmer.

Season the snapper fillets with more salt and black pepper to taste. Gently place the fish fillets into the simmering curry sauce. Spoon some of the sauce over the fish to coat it evenly. Add the potatoes, yam, dasheen and carrots to the simmering sauce and cook for 10–15 minutes until the vegetables start to become tender and the fish is cooked through and flakes easily with a fork. The cooking time will vary depending on the thickness of the fillets.

Serve the curry snapper with white rice or pasta.

Bajan Fish Cutter

SERVES 4

FOR THE FISH
450g (1lb) white fish fillets
    (such as cod or mahi-mahi)
1 lime or ½ lemon, juiced
Vegetable oil, for frying
½ tsp salt
1 tbsp ground black pepper
1 egg, beaten
1 tsp hot pepper sauce
10g (½oz) fresh parsley,
    finely chopped

FOR THE FLOUR MIXTURE
130g (4½oz/1 cup) plain
    (all-purpose) flour
1 tsp baking powder
½ tsp paprika
½ garlic powder
1 tsp ground black pepper
1 tsp salt

FOR THE CUTTER
4 sandwich rolls or Bajan
    salt bread rolls
Lettuce leaves
½ tomato, sliced
½ onion, sliced
¼ cucumber, sliced
4 gherkins
Hot pepper sauce or
    Bajan pepper sauce
Mayonnaise

The top memory I have from visiting Barbados was the fish cutter, served from a little hut by the bay. There was a constant queue to buy one – locals and tourists stood under the scorching sun waiting for a bite of the soft bun, the tomato juices flowing with the mayo, that little kick of pepper and then the saltiness of the fish. My goodness! Washing it down with a beer just topped the experience off.

Cut the fish fillets into smaller, sandwich-sized pieces. Place them in a bowl and drizzle with the lemon or lime juice. Season with the salt and black pepper and let them marinate for about 15–20 minutes.

Pour vegetable oil into a deep skillet or frying pan, so that it comes 1cm (½in) up the sides, and heat over medium-high heat.

In a shallow bowl, combine the whisked egg, hot pepper sauce and parsley.

In another bowl, combine all the ingredients for the flour mixture.

Dredge the marinated fish pieces first in the egg and then in the flour mixture, ensuring they are well coated.

Carefully place the coated fish pieces into the hot oil. Fry for about 3–4 minutes on each side or until they are golden brown and crispy. Remove the fried fish from the hot oil and place them on a plate lined with paper towels to drain any excess oil.

Slice the sandwich rolls or Bajan salt bread rolls in half horizontally. Layer lettuce leaves, sliced tomato, sliced onion, sliced cucumber and a gherkin on the bottom half of each roll. Place pieces of fried fish on top of the vegetables and add hot pepper sauce or Bajan pepper sauce and mayonnaise to taste. Top with the other half of the roll and serve immediately.

St. Lucian Green Fig + Salt Fish
Green Banana + Salted Codfish

SERVES 4

250g (9oz) salted codfish
   (salt fish)
4 green bananas
200g (7oz) yam, peeled
2 tbsp vegetable oil
1 onion, sliced
2 garlic cloves, minced
1 (bell) pepper, colour of
   your choice, deseeded
   and sliced
2 tomatoes, chopped
Salt and ground black pepper

This dish became so popular in the 19th century that it became the national dish of St. Lucia, where I am from. Green figs is the local name for green bananas. You can make it in bulk to feed the whole family and, as well as being delicious, it's super colourful and so looks great as well.

THE NIGHT BEFORE
Soak the salted codfish in cold water overnight or for a minimum of 5 hours.

ON THE DAY
Boil the salted codfish in a small saucepan of fresh water for 15 minutes then drain and set aside to cool. When cool, flake the salted codfish.

Cut both ends off each of the bananas and make a slit down the skin, being careful not to pierce into the banana flesh. Place the bananas in a pan of boiling water and boil for 15–20 minutes until the bananas are soft. Leave to cool, then peel the bananas and chop into 2½cm (1in) chunks.

In a separate pan, boil the yam for 15–20 minutes until soft. Leave to cool, then chop into 2½cm (1in) chunks.

In a saucepan, heat the vegetable oil over medium heat and sauté the onion, garlic and (bell) pepper for a few minutes until softened. Add the flaked, salted codfish and cook for a few minutes. Stir in the chopped tomatoes, cooked yam and the cooked green bananas and cook until everything is heated through. Season with salt and black pepper to taste and serve.

St. Lucian Breadfruit + Salt Fish Salad

SERVES 4

115g (4oz/1 cup) salted codfish
    (salt fish)
1 breadfruit
3 tbsp vegetable oil
1 onion, sliced
2 garlic cloves, minced
1 (bell) pepper, colour of your
    choice, deseeded and sliced
2 tomatoes, chopped
A squeeze of lime or lemon juice
Salt and ground black pepper

TO SERVE
Avocado, sliced
Fried Plantain (see page 38)

Breadfruit is one of the first dishes I look for when I go to St. Lucia as there's nothing like a freshly roasted or boiled breadfruit to accompany your breakfast or lunch. Breadfruit is a great alternative to potatoes as, depending on how you cook it, you can achieve a roast potato- or a boiled potato-like texture from it.

THE NIGHT BEFORE
Soak the salted codfish in cold water overnight or for a minimum of 5 hours.

ON THE DAY
Boil the salted codfish in a small saucepan of fresh water for 15 minutes then drain and set aside to cool. When cool, flake the salted codfish.

Wash the breadfruit and remove the stem. Bring a large pan of water to the boil, add the whole breadfruit and boil until tender, about 35–40 minutes. Drain in a colander and set aside to cool.

Slice the breadfruit into wedges. Pour 1 tablespoon of vegetable oil in a frying pan and place over a medium heat. Add the breadfruit and fry for 2–3 minutes on each side. Set aside.

Heat the remaining vegetable oil in the samer pan, add the onion, garlic and (bell) pepper and sauté for a few minutes until softened. Add the flaked, salted codfish and cook for a few minutes.

Stir in the tomatoes and cooked breadfruit and cook for a few minutes until everything is heated through. Season with salt, black pepper and a squeeze of lime or lemon juice.

Serve with avocado and fried or boiled plantain.

Haitian Black Bean Soup (VG)

SERVES 4

250g (1lb/2 cups) dried black beans
2 tbsp vegetable oil
1 onion, chopped
2 garlic cloves, minced
1 (bell) pepper, colour of your choice, deseeded and diced
2 carrots, peeled and diced
2 celery stalks, chopped
1 Scotch bonnet chilli, minced (or to taste)
1 tbsp ground cumin
1 tbsp ground coriander
1 tbsp fresh thyme leaves
2l (3½pt/8 cups) vegetable stock
250ml (9fl oz/1 cup) coconut milk
Salt and ground black pepper

TO SERVE
Hardo bread
Fresh flat leaf parsley, finely chopped

This is a hearty dish from Haiti, a velvety purée of beans and coconut milk, which is mainly eaten with white rice. It's a savoury dish and best made with dried beans rather than canned ones.

THE NIGHT BEFORE
Soak the black beans in a bowl of cold water overnight or for a minimum of 5 hours.

ON THE DAY
In a large pan, heat the vegetable oil over medium–high heat. Add the onion, garlic, (bell) pepper, carrots and celery and sauté for a few minutes until the vegetables have softened.

Drain the soaked black beans in a colander then stir in along with the Scotch bonnet, cumin, coriander and thyme leaves.

Pour in vegetable stock and bring to a boil. Reduce the heat, cover and simmer for 1½–2 hours, or until the black beans are tender.

Stir in the coconut milk and cook for a further 3–4 minutes, until warm through. Season with salt and black pepper to taste.

Serve the soup with hardo bread, scattered with the chopped parsley.

St. Lucian Callaloo Soup (VG)

SERVES 4

115g (4oz/1 cup) diced pumpkin
    or squash
1 tbsp vegetable oil
1 onion, chopped
2 garlic cloves, minced
100g (3½oz/1 cup) sliced okra,
    sliced
2 sprigs of fresh thyme
1 x 400g (14oz) can
    of coconut milk
1 litre (35fl oz/4 cups)
    vegetable stock
1 Scotch bonnet chilli, whole
1 bunch of callaloo leaves
    (substitute spinach
    if unavailable), chopped
Salt and ground black pepper

There is nothing better than a comforting callaloo soup on a cold winter's day. It's so easy to make and feels very healthy with the peppers, okra and fresh herbs, all simmered and blended into the callaloo to perfection.

Bring a large pan of water to the boil and then add the pumpkin or squash. Boil for 20 minutes until tender. Drain in a colander and set aside.

Heat the oil in a large saucepan over a medium heat, add the onion and garlic and sauté for a few minutes until translucent. Add the okra, pumpkin or squash and thyme and cook for a few minutes more.

Pour in the coconut milk and vegetable stock and add the whole scotch bonnet.

Bring to a boil, then reduce heat to medium–low and simmer for about 5 minutes, or until the vegetables are tender.

Add the chopped callaloo leaves and simmer until just wilted. Remove the Scotch bonnet and season with salt and black pepper before serving.

Tuna Salad

SERVES 2

2 x 140g (5oz) cans
of tuna in sunflower oil,
drained
100g (3½oz/½ cup) diced
pineapple
75g (2¾oz/½ cup) diced
cucumber
40g (1½oz/¼ cup) diced red
(bell) pepper
40g (1½oz/¼ cup) diced red
onion
1 tbsp chopped fresh parsley
Baguette, to serve

FOR THE DRESSING
1 tsp Jerk Seasoning (see
page 185)
2 tbsp Greek yoghurt
½ tbsp of lemon juice
½ tsp of dried chilli (red pepper)
flakes
Salt and ground black pepper,
to taste

When I'm stuck for lunch, I frequently revert to this dish as there's always a can of tuna in my cupboard and salad at the ready. It's fresh and filling and works on its own, as a filling for a sandwich, or with fried dumplins on the side.

In a large bowl, combine the tuna, pineapple, cucumber, (bell) pepper, red onion, and chopped fresh parsley.

Place all of the citrus dressing ingredients in a small bowl or jug and mix well. Season with salt and black pepper to taste. Drizzle over the tuna mixture and toss gently to combine.

Serve the tuna salad in a fresh baguette cut in half.

Prawn + Mango Salad

SERVES 4

16 large prawns (jumbo shrimp),
  peeled and deveined
2 tbsp Jerk Seasoning
  (see page 185)
375g (13¼oz/8 cups) mixed
  salad greens of your choice,
  such as finely sliced cos, little
  gem or iceberg lettuce,
  or rocket (arugula) leaves
2 ripe mangoes, peeled,
  and diced
1 avocado, diced
½ red onion, finely sliced
5g (⅛oz/¼ cup) fresh mint
  leaves, chopped

**FOR THE CARIBBEAN-STYLE
MANGO DRESSING**
½ mango, peeled and diced
½ lime, juiced
1 tsp malt vinegar
1 tsp extra virgin olive oil
Salt and ground black pepper

The easiest way to make you feel like you're on a sunny island by a beach is to knock up this dish. Barbecue the prawns, if you can, to give them that grilled smoky flavour.

Make the dressing by combining all the ingredients in a bowl. Season to taste with salt and black pepper.

Season the prawns with the jerk seasoning. Preheat a griddle pan or a large frying pan over a high heat and sear the prawns for about 3 minutes on each side, or until pink and opaque.

In a large salad bowl, combine the salad greens, mangoes, avocado, red onion and chopped mint leaves. Top with the grilled prawns.

Drizzle the mango dressing over the salad and toss gently to combine. Serve immediately.

Jerk + Pineapple Lobster Tail

SERVES 4

4 lobster tails
1 tsp Jerk Seasoning
  (see page 185)
1 pineapple, peeled, cored
  and sliced
Cooking oil spray
2 tbsp lime juice
1 tsp salt
120g (4¼oz/½ cup)
  tomato ketchup
4 tbsp honey
4 tbsp mirin
Fries, to serve

Lobster is a luxury in my house. It's reserved for date nights, birthday dinners and special occasions. When I do bring it out though, I mean business: jerk marinade, sweet grilled pineapple salsa, it truly is a party.

Coat the lobster tails in the jerk seasoning and leave to marinate for 30 minutes.

Preheat a griddle pan or large frying pan over a high heat until very hot. Spray the pineapple slices with cooking oil and add them to the griddle. Cook until char lines appear on the pineapple, about 3 minutes on each side. Dice the pineapple slices into chunks, then toss in the lime juice and salt.

Oil the still-hot griddle pan and lay the lobsters, flesh side down, on it. Cook for 6 minutes turning halfway through, until char lines appear on the lobster.

Meanwhile, in a saucepan over medium heat, combine the ketchup, honey and mirin. Cook for 4 minutes until warmed through. Toss in your grilled pineapple and stir to coat.

Serve your lobster tails with the pineapple salsa on the side and fries.

111

Quinoa Salad (VG)

SERVES 4

185g (6½oz/1 cup) quinoa,
    cooked
    and cooled
165g (6oz/1 cup) diced mango
170g (6oz/1 cup) cooked black
    beans, drained and rinsed
90g (3¼oz/½ cup) diced red
    (bell) pepper
40g (1½oz/¼ cup) diced red
    onion
¼ cup chopped fresh coriander
    (cilantro)
Caribbean-Style Mango
    Dressing (see page 108)
Salt and ground black pepper

This is light and nutritious, colourful and satisfying. If you're feeling like you've had too many rice dishes, then quinoa is a brilliant protein-packed substitute.

In a large bowl, combine the quinoa, mango, black beans, (bell) pepper, red onion, and fresh coriander.

Drizzle Caribbean-style mango dressing over the quinoa salad and toss gently to combine. Season with salt and black pepper to taste.

Steamed Fish

SERVES 4

4 snapper fish fillets (about 175–225g/6–8oz each), cleaned and scaled
1 tsp salt
1 tsp ground black pepper
½ tsp ground coriander
2 tbsp vegetable oil
1 onion, sliced
2 garlic cloves, minced
1 tbsp minced fresh ginger
1 Scotch bonnet chilli, finely sliced
2 tomatoes, chopped
1 red or green (bell) pepper, deseeded and finely sliced
1 carrot, peeled and finely sliced into matchsticks
50g (1¾oz/½ cup) sliced okra (optional)
2 limes, juiced
2 sprigs of fresh thyme

You can steam any type of fish, but choose a variety that doesn't break up easily when cooked so you still get a firm bite. In our household, you were only allowed to eat fish during Easter, so this would be served for lunch with hardo bread and I just couldn't get enough of it. In the Caribbean, this is served with breadfruit for breakfast or with water crackers and bammy for dinner.

Season the snapper fish fillets with the salt, black pepper and dried coriander. Set aside.

In a large, deep frying pan or a wide saucepan with a lid, heat the vegetable oil over medium heat. Add the onion, garlic, ginger and Scotch bonnet. Sauté for a couple of minutes until the onion becomes translucent.

Add the tomatoes, (bell) pepper, carrot and okra (if using). Sauté for another 3–4 minutes until the vegetables start to soften. Pour in 250ml (9fl oz/1 cup) water and add the lime juice. Stir to combine.

Place the seasoned snapper fish fillets on top of the vegetable mixture in the pan. Add the fresh thyme sprigs on top of the fish and cook for 15 minutes until cooked through and opaque.

Serve the fish with the vegetables.

04

SUNDAY SERVICE

Jerk Chicken

SERVES 4

4 tbsp Jerk Seasoning
   (see page 185)
2 tbsp olive oil
2 tbsp dark soy sauce
2 tbsp lime juice
4 chicken thighs or
   drumsticks

FOR THE COLESLAW
¼ red cabbage, grated
   (shredded)
2 carrots, peeled
   and finely sliced
2–3 tbsp mayonnaise
½ tbsp ground black pepper
½ tbsp salt

FOR THE SALAD
125g (4½oz) mixed salad greens
   of your choice, such as
   finely sliced cos, little gem
   or iceberg lettuce
½ cucumber, finely sliced
2 tomatoes, halved and sliced
1 large carrot, peeled and finely
   grated (shredded)
1 yellow (bell) pepper,
   deseeded and finely sliced
1 avocado, diced

FOR THE DRESSING
1 tsp vinegar
½ tsp dairy or oat milk
½ tbsp olive oil
¼ tsp ground black pepper
¼ tsp salt

TO SERVE
Rice + Peas (see page 139),
Fried Plantain (see page 38)

To me, real jerk chicken has to be made by the jerk (wo)man in a jerk pan. Preferably on the side of the road in Jamaica as well. Nothing is beating that jerk chicken; you can smell the smoky scent from a mile off. You can replicate the jerk flavours on a barbecue or even in your oven in this recipe, but if you are lucky enough to get over to Jamaica, seek out the real deal!

THE NIGHT BEFORE
In a bowl, mix together your jerk seasoning, olive oil, soy sauce and lime juice to create a marinade. Coat your chicken with the marinade and refrigerate overnight (or for at least 1 hour, if you're in a hurry).

ON THE DAY
Preheat a grill (broiler) to medium–high heat (or if you're lucky enough to have a jerk pan, heat one of those). Grill the chicken for 20–25 minutes, then turn the chicken and brush with marinade, and grill for a further 20–25 minutes. Brush with the marinade one last time and then grill for a further 10 minutes, until the outside is crispy and its cooked through.

While the chicken is cooking, combine all the ingredients for the coleslaw in a bowl and mix well to combine.

Prepare the salad ingredients and toss those together in another bowl.

In a small bowl or jar, stir together the ingredients for the dressing. Just before serving, drizzle over the salad and toss together.

Serve the chicken with the coleslaw and salad, with rice and peas and fried plantain on the side.

TIP
+ For an authentic charred jerk chicken experience, use a jerk pan or barbecue to cook your chicken, turning the meat frequently (every 10–15 minutes) and pouring jerk marinade over the chicken during turns. I spray quarter of a 330ml (11¼fl oz) bottle of lager evenly over the chicken about 10 minutes before the cooking time ends, for a smokier flavour.

Jerk Chicken Noodles

SERVES 4

225g (8oz) rice noodles
4 boneless, skinless chicken
   thighs, sliced into strips or
   leftover Jerk Chicken (see
   page 116)
2 tbsp Jerk Seasoning
   (see page 185)
3 tbsp vegetable oil
1 red (bell) pepper, deseeded
   and finely sliced
1 small pineapple, peeled,
   cored and diced
1 tbsp soy sauce
Lime wedges, to serve

Having leftover jerk chicken is always a bonus as there are so many dishes you can use it for in the days that follow. Jerk chicken noodles is one of those very quick wins – light and fun, colourful and bursting with flavour, it's makes a perfect, quick evening meal.

Cook the rice noodles according to packet instructions, then drain.

Put the chicken in a bowl and toss with the jerk seasoning to fully coat. Heat 1 tablespoon of the oil in a large frying pan over a medium–high heat and cook the chicken strips until browned and cooked through. Remove from the pan and set aside.

Heat the remaining vegetable oil in the same pan and stir-fry the (bell) pepper and pineapple until slightly caramelized. Add the chicken back to the pan along with the cooked noodles, and soy sauce. Toss everything together and serve with lime wedges for squeezing over.

Jerk Chicken Salad

SERVES 4

½ iceberg lettuce, roughly diced
½ mango, peeled and sliced
125g (4½oz) of fresh pineapple,
   roughly diced
Handful of pomegranate seeds
½ red onion, finely sliced
¼ yellow (bell) pepper,
   deseeded and finely sliced
180g (6¼oz) cooked
   Jerk Chicken, shredded
   off the bone (see page 116)
Jerk sauce

FOR THE VINAIGRETTE
2 tbsp white vinegar
4 tbsp extra virgin olive oil
¼ tsp Scotch bonnet chilli,
   minced
Splash of milk (optional)
Salt and ground black pepper

No jerk wastage, please! The tender love and care that goes into making a good jerk chicken means that all leftovers need to be reworked and served again. This salad is a gorgeous way to use up leftover jerk – the sweetness of pomegranate against the spice of the jerk is a party in your mouth.

In a large salad bowl, combine the lettuce, mango, pineapple, pomegranate, red onion and (bell) pepper.

Top with the shredded jerk chicken.

Combine all the ingredients for the Caribbean-style vinaigrette in a bowl. Drizzle over the salad and toss to combine. Finish with a drizzle of jerk sauce, to taste.

Sea Bass

SERVES 4

4 whole sea bass (about
   175–225g/6–8oz each),
   scaled, gutted and cleaned
   (ask your fishmonger to do
   this)
½ tsp salt
½ tsp ground black pepper
½ tsp chilli powder
½ tsp paprika
1 tbsp fish seasoning
½ tsp lemon
   pepper seasoning
1 onion, chopped
2 garlic cloves, minced
1 Scotch bonnet or habanero
   chilli, finely sliced
4 bay leaves
4 cloves
2 sprigs of fresh thyme
2 tbsp vegetable oil, greasing
1 tbsp unsalted butter
1 lemon or lime, juiced

Sea bass is a 'Top 3' fish for me. I buy the thickest ones I can find for a fuller experience. The trick here is to leave enough time to marinate and to ensure that you've stuffed the inside of that fish with the Scotch bonnet, onions, cloves, bay leaves and garlic for maximum flavour. You can couple this with salad, rice, mash potato – literally anything – and it will be filling and gorgeous.

Season the sea bass fillets with the salt, black pepper, chilli powder, paprika, fish seasoning and lemon pepper seasoning.

Combine the onion, garlic, Scotch bonnet or habanero, bay leaves, cloves and thyme sprigs to make a stuffing and use it to stuff the fish. Allow them to marinate for at least 30 minutes to absorb the flavours.

Preheat the oven to 180°C fan/200°C/400°F/Gas 6 and grease a baking tray with vegetable oil.

Carefully place the seasoned and stuffed sea bass onto the prepared baking tray, adding butter on top of each fillet. Bake for 20–25 minutes, depending on the size, until cooked through and opaque.

Spoon the juices over the fish to coat it evenly, then move the sea bass to the grill (broiler) for 5–10 minutes for that extra crispy finish.

Squeeze the juice of 1 lime or lemon over the cooked sea bass and serve.

Curry Goat

SERVES 4–6

2kg (4lb 8oz) goat meat,
   cut into pieces (ask your
   butcher for a mixture of
   shoulder, neck and leg)
4 tbsp Green Seasoning
   (see page 182)
4 tbsp Betapac
   curry powder
½ tbsp salt
1 tbsp ground black pepper
2 tbsp vegetable oil
1 tbsp dark brown sugar
2 onions, roughly chopped
3 garlic cloves, minced
1 tbsp grated fresh ginger
1 Scotch bonnet chilli, whole
½ tsp ground cumin
2 bay leaves
2 cloves
1 tbsp browning sauce
3–5 pimento seeds (allspice
   berries)
4 sprigs of fresh thyme
2 carrots, peeled and diced
2 extra large potatoes, peeled
   and cut into 5cm (2in) pieces
1 x 400g (14oz) can
   of coconut milk

TO SERVE
Coleslaw (see page 152)
Fried Plantain (see page 38)
Roti (see page 126) (optional)
White rice (optional)

Every single Sunday without fail, you will catch me cooking up a curry goat with white rice and coleslaw – it's an absolutely elite meal. I have no qualms about standing up for 3 hours for just one bite of this, every second is worth it. Adding coconut milk is not traditional, it's a personal touch I add to my curry goat to give the gravy a nice creamy texture and coconut aroma. If you have any curry goat left, I recommend trying it with roti (see page 126).

THE NIGHT BEFORE
In a large bowl, season the goat with the green seasoning, 2 tablespoons of Betapac curry powder, salt and black pepper, ensuring that the meat is fully covered. Cover the bowl and leave to marinate in the fridge overnight.

ON THE DAY
Heat the vegetable oil in a large cast-iron pan with a lid over a medium–high heat. Add the brown sugar and once it is bubbling, add the goat meat and sear for at least 3 minutes on each side until browned.

Add enough water to cover the goat then add the onion, garlic, ginger, Scotch bonnet, cumin, the remaining curry powder, bay leaves, cloves, browning sauce, pimento seeds and thyme. Cover with a lid and simmer for 1½ hours, stirring occasionally, and adding 235ml (8fl oz/1 cup) of water if it is looking dry or beginning to catch on the base of the pan.

When the meat is soft, add your carrots, potatoes and coconut milk. Cook for another 15–20 minutes, or until the vegetables are cooked and the goat meat is tender and nearly falling off the bone.

Serve the curry with coleslaw, plantain roti and/or white rice.

TIP
+ Ensure you always have enough water while your pot is simmering, checking every half hour, stirring and adding 235ml (8fl oz/1 cup) of water each time. This will also ensure your curry goat gravy is the right consistency at the end.

Roti
(V)

SERVES 4

260g (9¼oz/2 cups) plain
(all-purpose) flour
1 tsp baking powder
½ tsp salt
2 tbsp vegetable oil
Butter or ghee, for cooking
1 recipe quantity Curry Goat
(see page 124)

The only way to eat curry goat was with coleslaw and white rice... until I discovered it with roti. Picking up the goat in the roti and biting through the soft floured dough into juicy tender goat meat was just pure pleasure!

To make the roti dough, in a mixing bowl, combine the flour, baking powder and salt. Gradually add water and mix until a soft, pliable dough forms. Knead the dough for a few minutes until it's soft and stretchy, then divide the dough into 8 equal portions and roll them into thin circles using a rolling pin – aim for a diameter of about 20cm (8in).

Heat a large frying pan or flat griddle over medium–high heat and add a little butter or ghee. Place a roti on the heated skillet and cook for about 2 minutes on each side, or until it puffs up and turns golden brown. Set aside and repeat to cook all the roti.

To assemble, place a generous portion of curry goat in the centre of a roti. Fold the sides of the roti over the curry to create a square or rectangular shape and enjoy immediately.

Brown Stew Chicken

SERVES 4

1 onion, finely chopped
2 garlic cloves, minced
2½cm (1in) piece of fresh ginger, minced
½ Scotch bonnet chilli, minced
½ tsp smoked paprika
½ tsp dried thyme
½ tsp salt
½ tsp ground black pepper
2 tbsp olive oil
4 chicken thighs, bone in and skin on
2 tbsp vegetable oil
2 tbsp dark brown sugar
1 large green (bell) pepper, deseeded and roughly diced
1 large red (bell) pepper, deseeded and roughly diced
3 bay leaves
3–5 pimento seeds (allspice berries)
3 cloves
2 tbsp browning sauce
2 tbsp soy sauce
250ml (9fl oz/1 cup) chicken stock
White rice, to serve

Sweet, savoury and spicy... brown stew chicken is such a combo! This is one of the dishes I know I have to make double the amount of, so I can go again the next day for lunch. It's a filling dish, too, so great for get togethers.

THE NIGHT BEFORE
In a bowl, mix together the onion, garlic, ginger, scotch bonnet, paprika, thyme, salt, black pepper and olive oil. Coat your chicken with the marinade and refrigerate overnight (or for at least 1 hour, if you're in a hurry).

ON THE DAY
Heat your vegetable oil in a large frying pan over medium–high heat. Add the brown sugar and once it is bubbling, add the chicken thighs and sear for at least 3 minutes on each side, until browned all over. Remove from the pan and set aside.

In the same pan, sauté the (bell) peppers until they are soft.

Add the bay leaves, pimento seeds, cloves, browning sauce, soy sauce and chicken stock, then return the chicken to the pan and mix it all together. Cover and simmer on a medium heat for 30–40 minutes until the chicken is cooked through and the sauce consistency is to your liking.

Divide the stew between bowls and serve with white rice.

TIP
+ If your sauce is too watery, adding 1 tablespoon of cornflour (cornstarch) to it will help thicken the consistency. If your sauce is too thick, adding water, a cup at a time, will loosen it up.

Oxtail Stew

SERVES 4

250g (9oz/1¼ cups) dried butter (lima) beans
1kg (2lb 4oz) oxtail pieces
4 tbsp Jamaican Green Seasoning (see page 182)
2 tbsp soy sauce
2 tbsp browning sauce
1 tbsp vegetable oil
2 tbsp dark brown sugar
3 spring onions (scallions), sliced into 3, about 7.5cm (3in) long
3 (bell) peppers, colours of your choice, deseeded and sliced
4 sprigs of fresh thyme
3 pimento seeds (allspice berries)
3 cloves
2 bay leaves
1 Scotch bonnet chilli
1 tbsp tomato ketchup
½ tbsp salt
1 tsp ground black pepper

FOR THE SPINNERS
120g (4¼oz/1 cup) plain (all-purpose) flour

TO SERVE
Coleslaw (see page 152)
Potato Salad (see page 153)
White rice

Whew, the price of oxtail is admittedly criminal, but there's nothing like it so you just have to swallow the financial pill and get on with it! When you cook this until the meat is falling off the bone and it's all tender and juicy in your mouth, it's just incredible. Oxtail isn't complete without the butter beans and spinners, white rice and coleslaw and, similarly to curry goat, it's a dish you're guaranteed to see me cooking up on a Sunday.

THE NIGHT BEFORE
Soak the butter beans in a bowl of cold water overnight or for a minimum of 5 hours.

In a large bowl, season the oxtail with the green seasoning, soy sauce and browning. Cover and leave in the fridge overnight.

ON THE DAY
Heat the vegetable oil in a large cast-iron pan with a lid over medium–high heat. Add the brown sugar and once it is bubbling, add the oxtail meat and sear for at least 3 minutes on each side until browned all over.

Add enough water to cover the oxtail, then add the spring onions, (bell) peppers, thyme, pimento seeds, cloves, bay leaves and the Scotch bonnet chilli. Drain the butter beans and add to the pan. Bring to a simmer and cover. Cook for 2 hours, stirring occasionally and adding a splash of water if the meat starts sticking to the bottom of the pan.

To make the spinners, place the flour in a bowl with 115g (8fl oz/½ cup) water and knead until you have a soft, elastic dough. If the dough is too sticky, add a tablespoon more flour. Cover and set aside for 30 minutes.

Once the dough has rested, break off a thumb-sized piece and roll it between your hands until it is roughly the size of your middle finger. Repeat with the remaining dough.

Stir in the ketchup and the spinners and cook for a further 5 minutes until the oxtail meat is tender and nearly falling off the bone. Serve with coleslaw, potato salad and white rice.

Ginger + Garlic Glazed Salmon

SERVES 4

2 tbsp soy sauce
2 tbsp honey
2 tbsp minced fresh ginger
2 garlic cloves, minced
1 tsp hot pepper sauce
4 salmon fillets
½ tsp salt
1 tbsp ground black pepper
1 tbsp chilli and lemon pepper
2 tbsp vegetable oil

TO SERVE
Lime wedges (optional)
Pak choi, steamed
White rice

Salmon is a really versatile fish for me. I can make it in so many different ways but you can't beat a simple ginger and garlic marinade. Oozing with talent, this dish is impossible to get wrong.

In a bowl, whisk together the soy sauce, honey, ginger, garlic and hot pepper sauce. Set aside.

Season the salmon fillets with the salt, black pepper and chilli and lemon pepper. (For a stronger flavour, marinate overnight.)

In a large frying pan, heat the vegetable oil over medium–high heat. Add the salmon fillets and cook for 3–4 minutes per side, or until they are almost cooked through.

Pour the ginger–garlic glaze over the salmon and cook for an additional 1–2 minutes until the sauce thickens.

Serve the salmon with steamed pak choi, white rice and lime wedges, for squeezing over.

Curry Chicken

SERVES 3

2 onions, 1 roughly
    chopped and 1 sliced
2 garlic cloves, minced
1½ Scotch bonnet chillis
4 tbsp Betapac curry powder
½ tsp salt
1 tsp ground black pepper
¼ tbsp ground cumin
¼ tbsp ground turmeric
2 tbsp vegetable oil
1 tbsp demerara sugar
2 tbsp browning sauce
6 chicken thighs
1 x 400g (14oz) can
    of coconut milk
2 cloves
2 bay leaves
4 sprigs of fresh thyme
2 potatoes, peeled and cut
    into 5cm (2in) pieces
2 carrots, peeled and chopped
    into 2½cm (1in) pieces
White rice or Rice and Peas
    (see page 139)

I had this dish so much growing up as every Caribbean household would buss down a curry chicken. It ended up being one of the first things I tried to ace when I was teaching myself to cook. When I learned it, I cooked it pretty much every other day. I'm sure everyone was sick of me, but I couldn't stop showing it off – it was too good.

THE NIGHT BEFORE
In a blender, combine the roughly chopped onion with the garlic, half a Scotch bonnet, 2 tablespoons of the Betapac curry powder, the salt, black pepper, cumin, turmeric, 1 tablespoon of vegetable oil and 1 tablespoon of water. Blend to a purée, then pour over the chicken. Cover and leave to marinate in the fridge overnight.

ON THE DAY
Heat remaining 1 tablespoon of vegetable oil in a large pan over a medium–high heat. Add the sugar and browning sauce followed immediately by the chicken thighs and sear for 2–3 minutes until brown on both sides.

Add your can of coconut milk, the sliced onion, cloves, bay leaves, thyme, remaining Scotch bonnet, remaining Betapac curry powder, and enough water to cover the chicken. Simmer with a lid on for 20 minutes, stirring after 10 minutes to avoid the chicken sticking. Add your potatoes and carrots, and a splash more water if it's looking too thick, and keep an eye on it for the next stage of cooking. Cook for a further 15 minutes, until the chicken and vegetables are cooked through and the sauce has thickened.

Serve the curry chicken with white rice or Rice and Peas.

Lamb Chops

SERVES 4

8 lamb chops (about 900g/2lb),
   bone-in or boneless
2 tsp Jerk Seasoning
   (see page 185)
1 tsp ground allspice
1 tsp dried thyme
2 tbsp vegetable oil
1 onion, finely chopped
2 garlic cloves, minced
1 tbsp honey
Salt and ground black pepper
2 tbsp chopped fresh coriander
   (cilantro) or parsley, to
   garnish (optional)

My personal favourite thing to eat are lamb chops. Cooked right (medium), they're soft, juicy and oozing with flavour, and I always have to make double the amount because they seem to disappear off my plate far too quickly. These are best cooked and eaten fresh. I don't tend to refrigerate for use later, slightly 'cause they're too good to save for later but mainly as the texture is tougher when reheated.

If the lamb chops are bone-in, trim off any excess fat, or you can score the fat to prevent curling during cooking.

Season the lamb chops with salt and black pepper, the jerk seasoning, allspice and dried thyme. Rub the seasonings into the chops, then let them marinate for at least 30 minutes at room temperature, or longer in the refrigerator for a more intense flavour.

In a large frying pan, heat the vegetable oil over medium–high heat. Add the lamb chops and sear for 3–4 minutes on each side, or until they develop a golden-brown crust. You may need to work in batches to avoid overcrowding the pan. Remove the seared lamb chops from the pan and set them aside.

Add the onion and garlic to the same pan and sauté for a few minutes until the onion becomes translucent and fragrant. Return the lamb to the pan, drizzle over the honey and stir gently to incorporate the flavours. Taste and adjust the seasoning, adding more salt or jerk seasoning if desired.

Serve the lamb sprinkled with chopped fresh coriander or parsley, if using.

Rice + Peas
(VG)

SERVES 4

350g (12oz/2 cups)
   white long-grain rice
1 x 400g (14oz) can
   of coconut milk
50g (1¾oz/¼ cup) creamed
   coconut
1 x 400g (14oz) can
   of red kidney beans, drained
   and rinsed
2 garlic cloves, minced
2 onions, chopped
2 spring onions (scallions),
   cut into 3 pieces
2 sprigs of fresh thyme
½ tsp salt
1 tbsp ground black pepper
1 tsp all-purpose seasoning
½ tsp Betapac
   curry powder
2 bay leaves
2 cloves
½ Scotch bonnet chilli,
   minced

Being able to cook an excellent rice and peas is an extreme sport, so I've used long grain here as it's a better starter pack. Patience and trusting in your rice-to-water ratio are the keys to getting this right. If it's too wet, you've used too much water; if the rice grains are not completely cooked, you didn't use enough water. Don't panic if you don't get it right first time, just try and try again until you perfect it.

Rinse the rice until the water runs clear, then drain.

In a large pan with a lid over a medium heat, combine the coconut milk, creamed coconut red kidney beans, garlic, onions, spring onions, thyme, salt, black pepper, all-purpose seasoning, Betapac curry powder, bay leaves, cloves and Scotch bonnet. Cover and cook for 10 minutes.

Add the rice, add 300ml (10¼fl oz/1¼ cups) water then bring to a boil for a few minutes. Reduce the heat to low, cover, and simmer for 20–25 minutes, or until the rice is cooked and the liquid is absorbed.

Fluff with a fork before serving.

Escovitch Fish

SERVES 2

2 whole red snapper, scaled,
   gutted and cleaned (ask your
   fishmonger to do this)
½ tbsp salt
1 tbsp ground black pepper
2 tbsp all-purpose seasoning
½ tbsp smoked paprika
60ml (2fl oz/¼ cup)
   vegetable oil

FOR THE SAUCE
1 onion, finely sliced
2 garlic cloves, minced
1 Scotch bonnet chilli,
   finely diced
2 carrots, peeled and sliced
   into matchsticks
1 green (bell) pepper, deseeded
   and finely sliced
1 red (bell) pepper, deseeded
   and finely sliced
1 yellow (bell) pepper, deseeded
   and finely sliced
4 sprigs of fresh thyme
3–5 pimento seeds (allspice
   berries)
2 bay leaves
2 cloves
120ml (4fl oz/½ cup)
   white vinegar
1 tbsp dark brown sugar

When I was young, I was totally against snapper because of the amount of bones in the fish. But big up my mum, who taught me how to de-bone the fish in pretty much two knife flicks. Ever since then, I make escovitch often – it's quick and easy and super delicious.

THE NIGHT BEFORE
For the fish, in a bowl mix together your salt, black pepper, all-purpose seasoning and paprika. Season your fish on the inside and the outside with this mix, cover and leave to marinate overnight in the fridge (or for at least 1 hour, if you are in a rush!).

ON THE DAY
Heat the vegetable oil in a large frying pan over a medium heat and fry the fish until golden brown on both sides (about 4–6 minutes per side for a medium-sized fish). Remove from the pan and set aside.

For the sauce, add the onion, garlic, Scotch bonnet, carrots and (bell) peppers to the same pan and cook for a few minutes until slightly softened. Add the pimento seeds, thyme, bay leaves and cloves, then pour in the vinegar and brown sugar and bring to a simmer.

Once simmering, add your fish back into the pan and cook for a further few minutes, basting the fish with the vinegar sauce repeatedly till covered.

Serve the fish with some of the sauce spooned over the top.

Callaloo (VG)

SERVES 4

2 tbsp vegetable oil
1 onion, chopped
2 garlic cloves, minced
1 (bell) pepper, colour of your
   choice, deseeded
   and diced
1 x 400g (14oz) can of callaloo
   (or substitute spinach
   or collard greens, if not
   available)
1 x 400g (14oz) can
   of coconut milk
1 Scotch bonnet chilli, minced
1 tomato, diced
1 sprig of fresh thyme
½ tsp salt
1 tbsp ground black pepper

Callaloo is a plant used in many Ital dishes in the Caribbean. It's often mistaken for spinach, but it's much firmer in texture and tastes much stronger. Callaloo is a true superfood: adding this to your meal has so many health benefits, including boosting vitamin C intake and controlling your blood sugar level. Try to get as much of this in per week as you can.

In a large pan, heat the vegetable oil over medium–high heat. Add the onion, garlic and (bell) pepper and sauté for a few minutes until the onion is translucent.

Stir in callaloo (or greens), coconut milk, Scotch bonnet, tomato and thyme sprig, and season with the salt and black pepper.

Simmer for 15–20 minutes until the greens are tender and the flavours meld together.

Jerk Lamb

SERVES 8

1 lamb shoulder 2-3kg
   (4½-6½lb)
2 tbsp Jamaican Green
   Seasoning (see page 182)
2 tbsp Jerk Seasoning
   (see page 185)
5 garlic cloves
5 cloves
4 pimento seeds (allspice
   berries)
bunch of fresh thyme
1 tbsp vegetable oil
3 bay leaves

TO SERVE
Mashed potato (optional)
Vegetables of your choice
   (optional)

The trick to this is time: firstly, the marinade time – give the lamb as long as possible to soak up the jerk marinade; secondly, the cooking time – don't play with the cooking time to rush the process. Texture is important here so really stay patient, letting the lamb cook down slowly and basting it well in its juices.

THE NIGHT BEFORE
Season the lamb shoulder with the green seasoning and jerk seasoning, rubbing it all over to fully coat. Cut small slits all over the lamb using a knife and stuff the slits with garlic cloves and cloves. Cover and leave to marinate in the fridge overnight.

ON THE DAY
Bring the lamb shoulder up to room temperature. Preheat the oven to 160°C fan/180°C/350°F/Gas 4.

Cover a roasting tray with baking parchment and drizzle with the 1 tablespoon of oil. Add the lamb to the tray and slip the three bay leaves around it. Cover with foil and roast for 3 hours. Baste the lamb in its juices, uncover and cook for another hour until the lamb is so tender it's almost falling off the bone.

Serve with mashed potato and vegetables of your choice, if you like.

Jollof Rice

SERVES 6

6 tomatoes, roughly diced
2 onions, roughly diced
2 Scotch bonnet chillies,
  roughly diced
3 red (bell) peppers, deseeded
  and roughly diced
3 Romano peppers, deseeded
  and roughly diced
2 x 400g (14oz) cans
  of chopped tomatoes
175ml (6fl oz/¾ cup)
  vegetable oil
2 red onions, sliced
4 tbsp tomato
  purée (paste)
3 sprigs of fresh thyme
500g (1lb 2oz) long grain white
  rice, washed
2 stock cubes (vegetable
  or chicken)
1 tbsp paprika
2 tbsp all-purpose seasoning
3 bay leaves
1½ tbsp salt
1½ tbsp ground black pepper
Jerk Chicken (see page 116),
  to serve

I learned to make jollof rice from my Nigerian friend, and while it's a Nigerian dish I've had to confess it goes *down* with most meat dishes from the Caribbean. The tomato-based stew makes it a dish all on its own, but serving up jollof with jerk chicken, or any form of curry, just accompanies your meats on a new level.

Preheat the oven to 180°C/200°C/400°F/Gas 6. Put your chunks of tomato, onion, scotch bonnet, (bell) peppers and Romano peppers in a roasting pan and roast them for 30 minutes. Allow to cool a little, then transfer all the veg to a blender, along with your two cans of chopped tomatoes, and blend until smooth.

Heat 120ml (4fl oz/½ cup) of the vegetable oil in a large saucepan on high heat, then add your blended mixture – be careful as when this goes into your pan the oil may splash back and the mixture will very quickly bubble. Adjust the heat to medium–high, cover with a lid and let it cook for 20 minutes, checking frequently to stir your stew so it does not burn on the bottom of the pan.

While this is cooking, heat the remaining oil in a frying pan and add your red onions, tomato purée and thyme. Cook for 10 minutes on a high heat, until the onions are almost burned (this will add to the smoky flavour), then stir into your stew. Add your washed rice to the stew and stir.

In a separate saucepan, bring 375ml (13fl oz/1½ cups) of water to the boil, and add your stock cubes, paprika, all-purpose seasoning, bay leaves, salt and black pepper. Boil for 2–3 minutes, then add this to your stew and stir.

Cover the pot with foil and a tight lid and leave it to cook on a low heat for 20 minutes. Remove your lid and foil and stir the jollof with a fork. Replace the foil and lid and cook for a further 10 minutes. Give the rice a stir, but do not stir the burned bits at the bottom of the pan, just stir the rice at mid-top level.

Serve with jerk chicken, to combine the flavours of Jamaica and Nigeria.

Trinidadian Doubles (VG)

MAKES 6

260g (9¼oz/2 cups) chickpea (garbanzo bean) flour
260g (9¼oz/2 cups) plain (all-purpose) flour
½ tsp baking powder
1 tsp ground turmeric
1 tsp ground cumin
1 tsp ground coriander
1 tsp cayenne pepper
1 tsp salt
570ml (20fl oz/2½ cups) warm water
Vegetable oil, for frying
Tamarind chutney, mango chutney and/or hot sauce, to serve

FOR THE CHICKPEA TOPPING
340g (12oz/2 cups) cooked chickpeas (garbanzo beans)
2 garlic cloves
2 tsp ground turmeric
½ tsp salt
½ tsp ground black pepper

'Doubles' are a street food from Trinidad and Tobago consisting of two flatbreads filled with a curried chickpea filling. They are not too far away from the Caribbean Chickpea Curry with Roti (see page 86). Once I was introduced to this by a Trini chef I never looked back. I haven't made it to Trinidad yet, but it's high up on my list of places to visit for the food alone.

In a large mixing bowl, combine the chickpea flour, plain flour, baking powder, turmeric, cumin, coriander, cayenne pepper, salt and warm water to create a smooth dough. Let it rest for 30 minutes at room temperature.

Once rested, divide the dough into 6 portions. Roll each portion into a ball and press in the middle to flatten the doubles, so that they're about 10cm (4in) wide.

In a deep frying pan, heat the vegetable oil over medium–high heat. Place a piece of flattened dough into the pan and fry until golden brown on both sides, about 15–20 seconds on each side. Repeat, until you've used all of the dough.

Remove and drain on paper towels to soak up any excess oil.

Put the chickpeas in a saucepan with the garlic, turmeric and salt and black pepper. Heat through until piping hot.

To serve, divide your doubles between plates, top with a spoonful of the chickpeas and add your choice of chutney or hot sauce.

Coleslaw (V)

SERVES 4

2 carrots, peeled and grated (shredded)
½ cabbage, grated (shredded)
½ tsp salt
½ tsp ground black pepper
5 tbsp mayonnaise
1 tbsp salad cream
1 tsp of honey (optional)

Coleslaw is a traditional Caribbean salad that we serve on the side of most meat dishes. Sweet, crunchy and simple to make, it's always worth putting some time aside to knock one of these up to go alongside your main meal. You can use vegan salad cream or mayonnaise to make it plant-based.

Put the grated carrots and cabbage in a large bowl and stir together. Stir in the salt and black pepper, mayonnaise and salad cream. If you like your coleslaw extra sweet, add a teaspoon of honey.

Potato Salad
(V)

SERVES 4

6 large potatoes
4 tbsp mayonnaise
2 tbsp sour cream
1 tbsp salad cream
1 tbsp finely chopped fresh
  parsley
1 tsp mustard of your choice
½ tsp salt
½ tsp ground black pepper
70g (2½oz/½ cup) drained
  canned sweetcorn

Everyone makes potato salad in their own way, adding dill, peas, boiled eggs, etc., but I like to keep mine really simple, adding just sweetcorn. You can use vegan alternatives to make it plant-based. I like to cook my potatoes the morning of the day I'm planning to serve the salad, so that they have plenty of time to cool, and then make the salad shortly before serving.

Cut your potatoes into quarters, place them in a pan of water and bring them to boil on medium heat. Cook for 12–15 minutes or until tender. Drain and rinse under cold water to cool, then leave in the fridge for a couple of hours.

In a large bowl, mix together the mayonnaise, sour cream, salad cream, chopped parsley, mustard, salt, black pepper and sweetcorn. Mix in your cooled potatoes and leave in the fridge until you're ready to serve.

Roast Chicken

SERVES 4

1 whole chicken (about
    1.3kg/3lb)
2 tbsp Jamaican Green
    Seasoning (see page 182)
1 tsp salt
1 tsp tbsp ground black pepper
½ tbsp paprika
1 tbsp chicken seasoning
½ tbsp lemon
    and pepper seasoning
2 garlic cloves
¼ onion, chopped
½ Scotch bonnet chilli
2 cloves
2 bay leaves
1 handful of rosemary sprigs
3 sprigs of fresh thyme
1 apple
2 tbsp vegetable oil
1 tbsp unsalted butter
2 tbsp apple sauce
2 tbsp honey

Everyone loves a good old Sunday roast, but getting the chicken right is key – you don't want it dry and overcooked. I made this mistake the first few times I cooked it because I was scared the chicken wasn't cooked inside. Use a temperature probe to make sure it's 75°C (165°F) and baste it repeatedly so it stays juicy and you don't have the dry birds I did!

Preheat the oven to 160°C fan/180°C/350°F/Gas 4.

Season your chicken with the green seasoning, rubbing it all over the bird.

In a bowl, mix together the salt, black pepper, paprika, chicken seasoning and lemon and pepper seasoning. Season your chicken with this too, distributing it evenly over and inside your chicken. Stuff the inside of your chicken with the garlic, onion, Scotch bonnet, cloves, bay leaves, rosemary, thyme and an apple.

Place your chicken in a roasting tray, drizzle it with the vegetable oil and cover it with foil. Place the roasting tray on the middle shelf of the oven and leave your chicken to cook for 1 hour. After the hour, place the butter on top of your chicken. Mix the apple sauce with the honey and drizzle it onto and around your chicken. Base the chicken with its own juices and cook for a further 20 minutes with the foil removed until the chicken is golden brown and the juices run clear when the thickest part of the thigh is pierced with a skewer.

Rice + Lentils (VG)

SERVES 4

250g (9oz) dried red lentils
350g (12oz/2 cups) basmati rice
2 tbsp vegetable oil
½ onion, diced
½ spring onion (scallion), sliced
1 garlic clove, minced
¼ Scotch bonnet chilli, minced
1 x 400g (14oz) can
   of coconut milk
½ tbsp ground cumin
½ tbsp dried oregano
2 tbsp all-purpose seasoning
¼ tsp ground white pepper
½ tsp salt
2 sprigs of fresh thyme
1 bay leaf
2 cloves

A secret weapon, I'd only get this alternative to rice and peas on special occasions growing up. When I began to cook for myself, this was one of the dishes I knew I had to master so I could have it more frequently.

THE NIGHT BEFORE
Soak the lentils in a bowl of cold water overnight or for a minimum of 5 hours.

ON THE DAY
Rinse the rice until the water runs clear, then drain and set aside.

Heat the oil in a large saucepan with a lid over a medium–high heat and fry the onion, spring onion, garlic and Scotch bonnet and sauté for 5 minutes. Add the coconut milk, cumin, oregano, all-purpose seasoning, white pepper and salt and bring to the boil.

Drain the lentils then add to the saucepan with the sprigs of thyme, bay leaf and cloves and allow to boil for 15 minutes.

Add your washed, drained rice to the pan and add enough water to cover the rice and lentils by 2½cm (1in). Cover and simmer over a low heat for 12–15 minutes, or until the rice is cooked and the liquid is absorbed. Fluff with a fork before serving.

SUNDAY SERVICE MENU

Coleslaw
p.152

Jamaican Green Seasoning
p.182

Jollof Rice
p.148

Oxtail Stew
p.130

Potato Salad
p.153

Rice and Beans
p.139

Roast Chicken
p.154

05

SWEET TREATS

JULIE ADENUGA

Julie Adenuga is a British television and radio broadcaster and the creator and visionary of her own shows Don't @ Me and Julie's Top 5. She's a key voice in the music and entertainment industry — not just in the UK, but also in America (having previously been an anchor on Apple's Beats 1), and in Nigeria (where her parents are from). I met Julie at *Live Magazine* and we did everything together: created blogs about the UK scene; raved and documented grime sets across the country; and wrote about every and anything we came across for various magazines. Christmas 2010, we did a guest show on the iconic (and at that point unlicensed) underground station Rinse FM, which led to them drafting us in to have our own show. We both began our radio careers there, at a studio in Brick Lane in Shoreditch, East London.

After the radio show, Julie and I would head over to Nandos in Spitalfields and spend the whole day with our phones and laptops out, creating. We'd be there from opening to close, only being able to afford one meal each but taking comfort in the bottomless glasses of Coca Cola.

Julie was the first of our friendship group to become vegan. She described to me the difficulty back then: 'When I went vegan in 2012, I really stopped enjoying food; not being able to cook and being vegan is a death sentence. Nandos was the only restaurant I could go and find vegan food I liked – a chicken restaurant!' She exclaims. 'Veganism was self-enforced policing of food, because I had to think about what I was going to eat, and I don't really like salad. I enjoy vegetables but I'm not a salad fan at all.' From memory, I recall Julie always being somebody who enjoyed the social element of going out to eat (we were in restaurants all the time), but the eating food part… not so much. 'I'm eating because I have too, because if I don't I get a migraine' she laughs. 'When you get older and you're told official guidance on what you're supposed to be eating, you learn you need a balanced diet and you need particular items in your diet, so it takes the fun away from food.'

While it's no secret that a balanced diet is the way to go, it's not something that's often discussed in African or Caribbean households – growing up, you get what you're given, no questions asked. 'We could only afford to eat bread and stew at home: there were no vegetables, there was no meat… we used to take some bread out the bag, take two scoops of stew out the pot and dip the bread in the stew and eat it. That was my childhood memory of food. When it becomes about having a balanced diet, you're told to cut out palm oil cause it's bad for you, you're told items you've been eating your whole life could now give you cancer. Before you used to be able to rock up anywhere and get whatever was on the menu – that was fun to me, but food just got a bit serious'.

Julie refuses to cook; she'll tell you she 'can't' but having seen her conquer so many different areas of the unknown professionally, I'll stick with 'refuses to'. 'I can't cook,' she protests. 'I don't enjoy it, it's not fun, I don't know how to prepare all the food and there's too much washing up at the end. I'm not hungry by the time it's finished and I can't get the timing right so the food is all warm equally at the same time'. To be fair to Julie, these are the common reasons why one would not bother with cooking – it does require

'I have to have pepper in my food. Scotch bonnet sauce. Food needs to be spicy — not mild spice, but spice; that's the only way I can get into the flavour. If it's not spicy, I don't want it.'
— Julie Adenuga

a passion for food and patience … at the same time. Her solution? 'I eat delivered meals every day. It's expensive but the food is nice and delicious. I make my own breakfast, then I know I've got lunch and dinner prep to eat in the afternoon and evening. Then on Saturday and Sunday, I just hope someone rings me and asks me round to their house for dinner,' she laughs.

We share memories of going out, dining with friends, the time I went to a steak restaurant for my birthday and they dripped meat fat on the chips and sauteed the spinach in butter, so Julie (a vegan at the time) didn't have a single thing on the menu to eat (my bad, sorry Juls). 'Now I will eat anything … lamb shank with vegetables, broccoli and carrots and sweet potatoes' she sighs. 'Also an English breakfast and a roast dinner: they are elite. If I had to go into space like Sandra Bullock in Gravity, I'm asking for an English breakfast.'

It surprises me that her current favourites are British, since my recollection of Julie's house was that there was always a pot of jollof rice cooking, or stored in the fridge. 'Jollof rice is the greatest rice to touch down on road,' she nods. 'It's rice, so it fills you up, it's tasty cause it's made with tomato stew, and if you want to, you can add sweetcorn to it or chicken on the side - it just never lets you down. It's quite genius, actually.'

Living in a household with traditional Nigerian parents did shape Julie's taste buds in ways though. 'Ground rice, fufu, pounded yam - I could get down with all of those. One thing I avoided though was amala. It's black and just doesn't look very appealing. As a kid when you see that, it just looked like poo. So I avoided that, but it probably did just taste like ground rice,' she muses. Pepper is another key takeaway from growing up. 'I have to have pepper in my food. Scotch bonnet sauce. Food needs to be spicy - not mild spice, but spice: that's the only way I can get into the flavour. If it's not spicy, I don't want it.'

Guinness Punch

SERVES 4

1 x 330ml bottle of Guinness
250ml (9fl oz/1 cup) vanilla
   enriched milk (Nurishment,
   Alpro and Oatly all work well)
2 tbsp vanilla extract
½ x 397g (14oz) can
   of condensed milk
¼ tbsp freshly
   grated nutmeg
¼ tbsp freshly
   grated cinnamon
3 drops of Angostura bitters
Ice, to serve

Growing up, all the adults around me would drink Guinness Punch and I had to become of legal age before I could see what all the fuss was about. But it was worth the wait – and my goodness, what a delight.

Place all of the ingredients together in a blender and blend until well combined. Pour into tall glasses with ice and serve.

Peanut Punch

SERVES 4

500g (1lb 2oz) monkey nuts
100g (3½oz/1 cup) oats
235ml (8fl oz/1 cup) vanilla
  enriched milk (Nurishment,
  Alpro and Oatly all work well)
2 tbsp vanilla extract
½ x 397g (14oz) can of
  condensed milk
¼ tbsp freshly grated nutmeg
¼ tbsp freshly grated cinnamon,
  plus extra to serve

I wasn't allowed to drink this growing up because my mum's version contain's rum. Instead, my mum would make me this non-alcoholic version, but only once every four to five months as a treat. I would enjoy getting involved, peeling the monkey nuts and blending the mixture together – it's definitely a fun one to make with friends, children and family.

Peel your monkey nuts, then place them in a blender with all of the other ingredients.

Blend until there are no bits left and the drink is smooth. Keep refrigerated and use within 3 days.

Serve with an extra sprinkle of grated cinnamon.

Burnt Plantain Sundae

SERVES 2

1½ tbsp vegetable oil
1 plantain, cut into chunks
4 scoops of vanilla ice cream
20g (¾oz) crunchy
   toffee popcorn
2 tbsp toffee sauce

Plantain goes with everything as a main, but get the sweetest plantain and have it with toffee and ice cream and you'll find it's delicious as a dessert too. This is the sweetest of treats — and the naughtiest of them all!

Heat the oil in a frying pan over high heat and fry the plantain for a few minutes, turning over during cooking, until charred.

In two tall sundae glasses, layer up the ice cream, popcorn and charred plantain.

Drizzle with toffee sauce and serve.

Apple Crumble

SERVES 4

3 cooking apples, peeled,
    cored and sliced
2 tbsp caster (superfine) sugar
1 tbsp vanilla extract
Ice cream or custard, to serve

FOR THE TOPPING
175g (6oz/1⅓ cups) plain
    (all-purpose) flour
110g (3¾oz/½ cup plus
    1 tbsp) golden caster
    (superfine) sugar
110g (3¾oz/scant ½ cup)
    unsalted butter, cold, plus
    extra for greasing
1 tbsp rolled oats
1 tbsp demerara sugar

I truly believe a good apple crumble can go with any meal as dessert; coupled with vanilla ice cream or custard, there's not a dish I couldn't follow up with this. I like my crumble to apple ratio to be high – give me *allll* the crumble and a dash of apple.

Preheat the oven to 180°C fan/200°C/400°F/Gas 6. Grease a baking dish with butter.

Place the apples, caster sugar, vanilla extract and 1½ tablespoons of water in a saucepan and cook over a low heat until the apples have softened. Drain and transfer to the baking dish.

Put the flour, golden caster sugar and butter in a mixing bowl and rub the butter into the flour with your fingertips until the texture resembles coarse breadcrumbs. Stir in the oats, then sprinkle the crumble mixture over the apples in the dish. Sprinkle the demerara sugar on top.

Bake for 25–30 minutes until golden brown and bubbling. Serve with ice cream or custard.

Rum Punch

SERVES 4

125ml (4fl oz/½ cup) Wray
   and Nephew Overproof Rum
60ml (2fl oz/¼ cup) Appleton
   Estate dark rum
120ml (4fl oz/½ cup)
   strawberry syrup
120ml (4fl oz/½ cup) fruit punch
120ml (4fl oz/½ cup)
   pineapple juice
120ml (4fl oz/½ cup)
   orange juice
60ml (2fl oz/¼ cup) lime juice

TO SERVE
Ice
Lime wedges (optional)
Glace cherries, (optional)

You cannot go wrong with a classic rum punch. Any Caribbean occasion – birthday party, wedding, funeral – you'll find a huge jug of rum punch (or fruit punch for the kids). They key ingredient is pineapple, so don't hold back on the juices, and it's always best served ice cold.

Combine all of the ingredients in a large jug and stir well. Pour into tall glasses with ice and the fruit, if using, and serve.

Sprinkle Cake

SERVES 12

FOR THE CAKE
280g (10oz/1¼ cups) margarine
280g (10oz/1½ cups less 1 tbsp)
  caster (superfine) sugar
5 eggs
50ml (1¾fl oz/3 tbsp) milk
280g (10oz/2 cups plus 2 tbsp)
  self-raising (self-rising) flour
2 tsp vanilla extract

FOR THE TOPPING
350g (12oz/2½ cups) icing
  (confectioner's) sugar
3–4 tbsp boiling water
Rainbow sprinkles

This is the first cake I learned to make when I was at school. I would count down the days to cooking class and pray that it was sprinkle cake. The days that we had sprinkle cake for lunch were my happiest days at school. Maybe everyone was so much more energetic because it is so full of sugar!

Preheat the oven to 160°C/180°C/350°F/Gas 4. Line a 23 x 30 cm (9 x 12in) cake tin with baking parchment.

Cream together the margarine and sugar until fluffy. Add the eggs one by one, mixing well after each addition. Add the flour, milk and vanilla extract, and mix again until you have a smooth batter.

Put the batter into your baking tin. Bake in the preheated oven for 30–40 minutes until risen and golden and a skewer inserted into the centre of the cake comes out clean. Leave to cool in the tin for a few minutes, then transfer to a wire rack to cool completely.

The next day, mix the icing sugar and boiling water together in a bowl until you have an icing with a thick pouring consistency. Pour the icing onto your cake and scatter over some rainbow sprinkles. Leave to set, slice into squares, and serve.

Jam Tarts

MAKES 12

175g (6oz/1¹/₃ cups) plain
    (all-purpose) flour, plus
    extra for dusting
1 tbsp caster (superfine) sugar
85g (3oz/¹/₃ cup plus 2 tsp)
    unsalted butter, cold and
    cubed, plus extra for greasing
1 medium egg yolk
1 tsp vanilla extract
1–2 tbsp cold water
125g (4½oz/½ cup) raspberry,
    strawberry, blackcurrant or
    apricot jam (jelly), or lemon
    curd

I'm an old-school girl when it comes to desserts; I want sweet and sticky and edible bites. I grew up on jam tarts and I enjoy making them now because I can use all the bits and bobs that are already in my kitchen cupboard.

Preheat the oven to 180°C/200°C/400°F/Gas 6. Grease a 12-hole tart tin with butter.

To make the pastry, sift the flour and salt into a bowl. Add the butter and rub it into the flour using your fingertips until it looks like breadcrumbs. Stir in the egg yolk and vanilla with a round table knife, then add as much of the cold water as you need to bring the mixture together to form a dough. Gather the dough into a ball, wrap it in cling film (plastic wrap) and leave to chill in the fridge for 30 minutes.

On a floured surface, roll out the pastry until it's 5mm (¼in) thick. Use a round 7cm (2¾in) cutter to stamp out 12 circles of pastry, then press one disc of pastry into each hole of your tart tin, pushing it down gently.

Spoon a heaped teaspoon of jam or curd into each pastry case. Bake in the oven for 15–18 minutes or until the pastry is golden brown.

06 SE

ASONINGS, SAUCES AND RUBS

Jamaican Green Seasoning

MAKES 1 SMALL JAR

Leaves from 1 bunch of fresh
   thyme, leaves picked
1 bunch of fresh parsley, leaves
   and stems
4 spring onions (scallions),
   sliced
4 onions, peeled
4–6 garlic cloves, peeled
2 sticks celery, roughly diced
1–2 Scotch bonnet chillies,
   deseeded (adjust to taste and
   spiciness preference) and
   roughly diced
1 green (bell) pepper, deseeded
   and roughly diced
1 red (bell) pepper, deseeded
   and roughly diced
1 lime or lemon, juiced
1 tbsp white vinegar or apple
   cider vinegar
1 tsp ground allspice
1 tbsp olive oil

Keep some of this in your fridge in a sterilized and sealed glass jar. It will store for up to 3 weeks if sealed properly. You can use it for marinades, or stir a spoonful into whatever you're cooking to give it a flavour boost. I supplement powdered seasoning for green seasoning most of the time.

Wash and clean all the fresh herbs thoroughly. Place all the ingredients in a blender or food processor and pulse until you achieve a smooth and vibrant green paste. You may need to add up to 120ml (4fl oz/½ cup) water gradually to achieve the desired consistency.

Transfer the green seasoning to a sterlized airtight container or jar. It can be stored in the refrigerator for 1–2 weeks. To preserve it for longer you can freeze the blend – it lasts for up to 3 months in the freezer.

Jerk Gravy

MAKES 1 SMALL JUG

2 tbsp vegetable oil
1 onion, finely chopped
2 garlic cloves, minced
2 tsp Jerk Seasoning
   (see page 185)
½ tsp ground allspice
½ tsp dried thyme
½ tsp paprika
235ml (8fl oz/1 cup) chicken or
   vegetable stock
235ml (8fl oz/1 cup) coconut
   milk
1 tsp ground black pepper
1 tsp salt
1 tbsp cornflour (cornstarch)
   (optional, for thickening)

It's always good to have a jerk gravy on hand to cover pretty much any dry (think flour-, rice-, or potato-based dishes) meal with. It works especially well on a good old Sunday roast.

In a saucepan, heat the vegetable oil over medium heat. Add the onion and garlic and sauté for 2–3 minutes until the onion becomes translucent and fragrant.

Add the jerk seasoning, allspice, thyme and paprika to the pan and stir to coat the spices with the oil. Cook for another 1–2 minutes to release their flavours.

Pour in the chicken or vegetable stock and coconut milk. Stir well to combine. Bring the mixture to a gentle simmer, then reduce the heat to low. Let it simmer for about 10–15 minutes to allow the flavours to meld.

If you prefer a thicker gravy, mix the cornflour with a splash of water to make a slurry. Slowly pour the slurry into the simmering gravy while stirring continuously. Continue to simmer for a few more minutes until the gravy thickens to your desired consistency. If it becomes too thick, you can thin it with a bit of water.

Remove the jerk gravy from the heat. Serve with roast meats and vegetables.

Jerk Seasoning

MAKES 1 SMALL JAR

4–6 Scotch bonnet chillies
(adjust to taste and spiciness
preference)
6–8 spring onions (scallions),
sliced
4–6 onions, peeled and
chopped
4–6 garlic cloves, minced
2 tbsp fresh thyme leaves (or
2 tsp dried thyme)
2 tbsp ground allspice
2 tbsp dark brown sugar or cane
sugar
1 tbsp ground black pepper
1 tbsp ground cinnamon
1 tbsp ground nutmeg
1 tbsp ground ginger
1 tbsp salt, or more to taste
2–3 tbsp vegetable oil or olive
oil
2 tbsp soy sauce
2 tbsp white vinegar
1–2 limes, juiced
1 tsp ground cloves
1 tsp ground cayenne pepper
(optional, for extra heat)
1 tsp paprika

Have one jar of jerk seasoning in your fridge at all times: it will store for up to 3 weeks if contained properly. This is not only used for marinades but can be spooned into your dishes while cooking to give an extra kick of spice, particularly for the cinnamon, ginger and soy.

Place all the ingredients in a blender or food processor and blitz until you achieve a smooth paste. You may need to scrape down the sides of the blender or food processor to ensure everything is well combined.

Taste the jerk seasoning and adjust the spiciness and salt to your preference by adding more Scotch bonnet or salt if needed.

Transfer the jerk seasoning paste to a sterilized, airtight container or jar. It can be stored in the refrigerator for up to 3 weeks. To preserve it for longer you can freeze the blend – it lasts for up to 3 months in the freezer.

A—Z of Seasonings

A quick reference guide to the main seasonings I use throughout the book.

ALLSPICE (PIMENTO): A fundamental spice in Caribbean cuisine, it has a warm and slightly sweet flavour with hints of cinnamon, nutmeg and cloves. Ground allspice is used in rubs, marinades and stews.

BASIL: Fresh basil leaves are used in Caribbean dishes, particularly in pesto-like sauces and herbaceous seasonings.

BAY LEAVES: These aromatic leaves are used to season stews, soups and rice dishes, imparting a subtle herbal note.

BETAPAC CURRY POWDER: Betapac or Jamaican curry powder is used in Caribbean cuisine, particularly in Trinidad and Guyana, to season dishes like curry chicken and curry goat.

BROWNING SAUCE: A caramel-coloured sauce used to give dishes a rich, dark colour. It's often used in stewed meats and rice and peas.

COCONUT MILK: Coconut milk is often used to add a creamy texture and a mild sweetness to various Caribbean recipes, such as curries, soups and rice dishes.

CORIANDER (CILANTRO): Fresh coriander leaves are used as a garnish in many dishes, adding a burst of fresh flavour.

CHILLI POWDER: Chilli powder adds spiciness and depth of flavour to Caribbean dishes, especially when you want to increase the heat.

CINNAMON: Ground cinnamon is used in desserts, baked goods and some savoury dishes for its warm and sweet aroma.

CUMIN: Ground cumin adds an earthy and smoky flavour to spice blends and curries.

CLOVES: Whole or ground cloves are used in Caribbean recipes, especially in holiday dishes like sorrel and baked ham.

GARLIC: Garlic is a staple in Caribbean cooking, used to season a wide variety of dishes from meats and seafood to rice and vegetables.

GINGER: Fresh ginger root is used for its warm and zesty flavour. It's used in marinades, sauces and soups, as well as in beverages like ginger beer. Fresh ginger is used to add a hint of warmth and a spicy kick to dishes.

GREEN SEASONING: A blend of fresh herbs and spices, including coriander (cilantro), spring onions (scallions), thyme and garlic. It's used as a marinade or seasoning paste for meats, fish and poultry. (See page 182 for my recipe.)

JERK SEASONING: A blend of spices including allspice (pimento), spring onions (scallions), thyme, garlic and Scotch bonnet chilli, jerk seasoning is used to marinate and season meats, giving them a smoky, spicy flavour. (See page 185 for my recipe.)

LEMON PEPPER SEASONING: Lemon pepper seasoning combines the zestiness of lemon and the mild heat of black pepper, offering a zesty and spicy flavour to various dishes.

LIME AND LEMON JUICE: The juice of these citrus fruits is used to add a tangy and refreshing element to various dishes.

NUTMEG: Freshly grated nutmeg is used to season dishes like sweet potato pudding and desserts. It has a warm, sweet and slightly spicy flavour.

ONION: Onions are used as a base in many Caribbean dishes to add depth of flavour to the dish.

PARSLEY: Fresh parsley is used as a garnish to add colour and freshness to many Caribbean dishes.

PAPRIKA: Smoked paprika or sweet paprika is used to season meats, poultry and seafood, adding a subtle smokiness and colour.

SCOTCH BONNET CHILLI: These fiery hot peppers are a staple in Caribbean cooking. They add intense heat and a fruity flavour to dishes and are often used in marinades, sauces and soups. Use them sparingly and be cautious when handling them.

SESAME OIL: Used in stir-fry dishes and sauces for its nutty and aromatic flavour.

SOY SAUCE: In some Caribbean cuisines, especially in Trinidad, soy sauce is used to add a savoury umami flavour to dishes.

THYME: Fresh or dried thyme is commonly used to season meats, stews and soups. It adds a subtle earthy and aromatic note to dishes.

VINEGAR: Vinegar, especially white or malt vinegar, is used in pickling and to provide acidity to dishes like escovitch fish.

PLAYLISTS

01
20 MINUTES

Kraff Gad
Calmc

Valliant
Dunce Cheque

Popcaan
Buzz

Skillibeng
Crocodile Teeth

Alkaline
Champion Boy

T.O.K
She's Hot

Dexta Daps
Shabba Madda Pot

Aidonia
Yeah Yeah

Teejay
Drift

Baby Cham
Vitamin S

02
COMFORTS

I Wayne
I Need Her In My Arms

Mr Vegas
I Am Blessed

Sizzla
Solid As A Rock

Kranium ft Idris Elba + Tanik
Stand By Me

Bob Marley
Could You Be Loved

Amaria BB
Slow Motion

Singing Sweet
When I See You Smile

Alaine
Make Me Weak

Chaka Demus + Pliers
Murder She Wrote

Gyptian
Hold You

03
FROM THE ISLANDS

Krosfyah
Pump Me Up

Patrice Roberts
Mind My Business

Collie Buddz
Mamacita

Demarco
I Love My Life

Edwin Yearwood
Wet Me

Peter Ram
Good Morning

Machel Montano
Fast Wine

Freezy
Split In The Middle

**Skinny Fabulous, Machel Montano
+ Bunji Garlin**
Famalay

04
SUNDAY SERVICE

Beres Hammond
Rockaway

Sanchez
Missing You

Morgan Heritage
She's Still Loving Me

Tarrus Riley
She's Royal

Dennis Brown
Here I Come

Richie Spice
Brown Skin

Gappy Ranks
Heaven In Her Eyes

Jah Cure
That Girl

Freddie McGregor
I Was Born A Winner

Garnett Silk
Oh Me, Oh My

05
SWEET TREATS

Beenie Man + Janet Jackson
Feel it Boy

Pressure
Love and Affection

Buju Banton
Wanna Be Loved

Sean Paul + Cecile
Can You Do The Work

Tanto Metro + Devonte
Everyone Falls In Love

Chronixx
Skankin' Sweet

Wayne Wade
I Love You Too Much

Serani
No Games

Terror Fabulous + Nadine Sutherland
Action

Wayne Wonder
No Letting Go

06
SEASONINGS, SAUCES AND RUBS

WSTRN
Ben Ova

Lady Saw
Man Is The Least

Dexta Daps
Call Me If

Spice
So Mi Like It

Shenseea + DJ Frass
Good Comfort

Sneakbo
Touch A Button

Stylo G
Dumpling

Alicai Harley
Put It On You

Big Zeekz
Happy

IQ
Bun Fi Bun

INDEX

THANK YOU

The first thank you goes out to my friend the late Jamal Edwards. He spoke so highly of me to his then agent Crystal Mahey-Morgan, that from 2016 right through to 2021 she was in my DM's with words of affirmation about my writing skills and advice about my self published cook book. Unbeknown to him, that led me to this point, to me releasing this book with Crystal as my agent. Jamal you're a legend, you will never be forgotten for the lives you positively impacted, love you always <3

Crystal, thank you for your undeterred belief in me, even from afar and before we'd ever met. Being a part of the OWN IT! family with yourself and Jason has been a pleasure from the get go and I wouldn't have been able to do this with anyone else.

Eleanor and Charlotte, Stephanie and the whole Quarto team, thank you for inviting me into Carnival and seeing the vision for Sian's Kitchen, thank you for pulling it all together even though I am an absolute nightmare to get hold of (sorry). Thank you for your patience and expertise, I am so proud of this book and how it came to exist.

My team at Octaves, thank you for holding it down while I was off shooting this book. Alex, Shiezel, Cynthia (my mum) and the food safety inspector at Hackney Council (if you know you know).

Ella Bonai-Gordon my sister, Big Zuu, Julie Adenuga, Big Narstie and Sharlene, Vicky Grout (you will always be my one and only shooter <3) and everyone else who made the interviews and photos happen.

Love to all of my pals who gave me the daily encouragement I needed to get this done (Caitlyn mainly looking at you).

And finally, to Ella Miller (photography) and Christina Mackenzie (food stylist) – you are exceptional at what you do! Your love for it, your passion for food, your attention to detail, level of professionalism... I could go on and on about you both and the dream teams you pulled together to assist the shoot days. I had so much fun shooting this with you guys, you brought this to life for me for real for real! Thank you.

Lucy on design, the cover is STRIKING – thank you <3

And finally finally (really finished this time) thank you to everyone who picked up this book, I hope you enjoy putting it to good use and I hope it brings you the same joy that cooking brings to me.

Omg I'm super emotional basically THANKS SO MUCH TO YOU ALL LOVE YOU BYE XXX

ABOUT SIAN

Sian Anderson is a media powerhouse and restaurateur. Alongside running her own restaurant, Octaves, Sian also broadcasts on BBC Radio 1Xtra every Saturday and has a specialist DJ show on Mondays. She is also the presenter of Channel 5/BET's *Big Money Munch*, a culinary journey to uncover and celebrate the best Black-owned eateries in the UK.

Sian's kitchen has always been a space for connection and gathering. Her passion for food is grounded in sharing a meal with others for nourishment and enjoyment. She also took her mate Ed Sheeran's advice and opened Octaves, a modern Caribbean restaurant in London in September 2023.

Her first self-published cookbook, *Sian and Her Son,* and was published in lockdown in 2021. The book features the cooking Sian and her son, Elijah, bonded over during the pandemic and includes delicious recipes for both adults and children.

Recipe icons denote the following
VG = Vegan
V = Vegetarian

Quarto

First published in 2024 by Carnival
an imprint of The Quarto Group.
One Triptych Place, London, SE1 9SH
United Kingdom
T (0)20 7700 6700
www.Quarto.com

A catalogue record for this book is available from the British Library.

ISBN 978-0-7112-9254-3
EBOOK ISBN 978-0-7112-9255-0

10 9 8 7 6 5 4 3 2 1

Book Designer: Studio Polka
Editor: Charlotte Frost
Editorial Director: Nicky Hill
Food and Prop Stylist: Christina Mackenzie
Food Styling Assistants: Jess Geddes and Lauren Wall
Food Photographer: Ella Miller
Food photographer's Assistant: Rose Mordaunt
Personality Photographer: Vicky Grout
Publisher: Eleanor Maxfield
Senior Designer: Isabel Eeles
Senior Production Manager: Eliza Walsh

Printed in China